Ghosts, *Critters* & Sacred Places Of Washington and Oregon

By Jefferson Davis

First Printing 1999

Although the author has researched all sources to ensure the accuracy and completeness of the information contained within this book, he assumes no responsibility for errors, inaccuracies, omissions or inconsistency herein. Nor does the author presume to pass judgement as to the truth of any paranormal events or stories contained within. Any slights of people or organizations are unintentional.

Printed by Gilliland Printing, Arkansas, Kansas

Library of Congress Number: 98-90574
Davis, Jefferson Dale
Ghosts, Critters & Sacred Places of Washington and Oregon
1. Native Americans
2. Spirituality and Mythology
3. Local History
4. Includes Index
ISBN: 1-893186-02-4

Acknowledgments

Thank you, Mr. Doug Clark of the *Spokesman-Review*. Thanks to all of the managers and employees of the various McMenamins establishments. I wish to give a special thanks to Tim Hills of McMenamins for his help and historic consultations.

Thank you Red Elk for your story and insight. On the technical end, thank you Sue, Andrea and mom for proofing the draft of this book. Thanks Zen-website-guru John Goodman for your tireless upgrades of my homepage. Thank you Su at Septagon Graphics for the great cover art.

Thanks to all of the people who liked my first book well enough to buy this one!

Preface

Welcome to my second book, *Ghosts, Critters and Sacred Places of Washington and Oregon*. One of the things that I hate when I read a book is finding out that I have to buy the previous (or next) book to get the whole story. I know I am not alone. My first book included several stories from locations mentioned in this book. That is because as time goes on, haunted buildings remain haunted and more stories accumulate. In this book when I return to an old location or haunted house, I have new information. I have tried to strike a balance between giving enough information to readers of this book to understand the nature of the hauntings but not repeat the original story in such detail that people feel cheated.

All cultures of the world believe in an afterlife and ghosts. How does our culture relate to our ghosts on a social and spiritual level? Ghost stories and legends can explain things we don't understand. Stories with ghosts usually have a moral that reinforces a positive message for society. They are also entertaining. They may scare us, but they excite us as well. When our bodies die, do we cease to exist? Under certain circumstances can we imprint the memory of a feeling, aura or event in a certain place? Is this really part of us, with our memories or is it just a recording. We are only now exploring the power of the human mind.

There is natural phenomena that are mistaken for the paranormal that includes things like earthquakes or underground water can make strange noises and buildings shake. There is also the wonder and magic of the human mind and body. What makes a place sacred? Is there some power that has resided there since the dawn of time, or do people gathering there in worship and ritual give power to these places.

I would like to be able to discuss all of this in one comprehensive volume but I have been forced to do this in installments. In this book I focus on the Puget Sound and Willamette Valley as well as Eastern Washington and my hometown of Vancouver, Washington. Many of these locales are open to the public so feel free to visit them, except where I have a warning requesting no visitors.

If you have stories that you would like to tell, please write to me at Ghost Stories, PO Box 4803, Vancouver, WA 98662 or contact me at jddavis@rocketmail.com.-Jeff Davis

Table of Contents

Introduction

This book is divided into broad categories. There are stories of Native American ghosts and hauntings. Many of these are naturally located on or near sacred sites and graveyards. Native American worship has continued at ancient site into modern times. In addition to ancient sites, new age or pagan practices have begun at some old and new locations. These stories are found both in the section on Native American ghosts as well as scattered throughout the book. There are also several stories about modern ghosts from across Washington and Oregon as well as a section on the various mythological and not so mythological "critters" of the Pacific Northwest.

What is a ghost? A recent study I have heard cited says that at least 25% of the people in America believe in ghosts. Ten percent of Americans believe that they have had ghostly encounters. Other people do not believe in ghosts and that is the end of the discussion. Other people have different theories as to what causes the phenomena we commonly refer to as ghosts. Still other people are curious and unconvinced and wait for more information. For these people I will try and give a brief background on the paranormal phenomena of ghosts and hauntings.

The simplest definition of a ghost is; A ghost is the spiritual remains of a deceased person that remains on earth instead of passing on to a different plain of existence. Not a simple definition is it? Another definition is that a ghost is basically a soul without a body. It can manifest itself in many paranormal ways, such as being seen, heard, felt, touched or even smelled. A haunting should be defined as several paranormal events in a common setting.

Most hauntings are associated with buildings or places. In some cases, when the buildings are torn down, the haunting ceases. In other cases, the hauntings continue in the vacant lot or new structure. This happened to a family who set up a mobile home on a pasture in Battle Ground, Washington. The haunting may not be tied to a location. It could be tied to a person or thing. Poltergeists are usually attached to children and follow them from place to place. Mythical curses follow people around. There are also examples of haunted houses being moved and the ghost moves with them. Some ghosts seem to be attached to certain objects, such as a picture of an older couple that a friend of mine picked up at a garage sale. But that is another story.

One of the questions about ghosts is, why do we see them mostly at night? Aren't they there during the day? Maybe they are and we just don't perceive them as such. If ghosts are solid looking, we may think that they are living beings. We may just look at them differently if we see them in places they should not be, like a dark, empty building. Then again, we may still see ghosts in unexpected places and times and still treat them as living beings because they are still carrying on business as usual. Like night watchmen following their old rounds or soldiers waiting to ship out, as in a case at the Vancouver Barracks.

A very common type of ghost that usually does not lead to a haunting is the apparition of a living person. In times of war or natural disaster the number of reports of this type of phenomena increase. A person wakes up in the middle of the night to see a spouse or loved one, standing beside their bed. The figure may say goodbye or just look at them and then disappear. Some days or weeks later the sleeper finds out that their loved one has died. In other cases, the person whose apparition was seen is still alive, though stressed. After this single occurrence the apparition usually does not appear again.

The most common type of ghost seems to be a kind of snapshot in time. Frequently, violent or traumatic events seem to release an energy that imprints the action on a place or object. In this kind of haunting, the violent action repeats itself, like videotape rewound and played over and over again. Sometimes it is not violent action. It can also be the result of someone performing the same actions over and over again in life, that somehow imprint themselves on a place after the person is dead or gone.

These hauntings can be seen, heard, felt or even smelled. Ghosts are frequently seen at the same time every night, or at certain seasons of the year. They are not doing anything remarkable, they are just going about their business, like a maid cleaning rooms or a night watchman making his rounds. The ghosts are not aware of their surroundings, just as in a movie. That is why some ghosts appear walking though solid walls, where there used to be a doorway. They may also walk above or below a modern floor. Their surroundings have changed but the ghosts have not. Sometimes if people concentrate on an apparition of this kind, the ghost can perceive them. Hospitals are frequently haunted by the actions of the trauma, pain and fear that goes on within their walls. Some spirits stay on for a reason we cannot understand.

The self-aware spirit of a person is another kind of haunting. In this case, spirits continue to exist in places where they lived or worked, after their death. These spirits often stay on because they have business that they want to finish. Sometimes they want to pass on information about their life, death or something more important than life itself (to them). They may be waiting for a friend, even after death. There are guardian spirits, who protect a secret or perhaps treasure. They may have suffered a tragedy in the past and want to warn others in similar circumstances. Some spirits stay on for no apparent reason like poltergeists.

Poltergeists are "*noisy ghosts*". They are quite evident because they cause things to move from place to place, make noise and generally upset the routine of their surroundings. Poltergeists are usually associated with children before or during puberty. Poltergeists usually fade as puberty ends. This is the kind of ghost that seems to be faked most often by people.

Most ghosts seem to fade away over time. They are most energetic after whatever event creates them. As time goes by their manifestations become less frequent. At first some ghosts are seen, heard and felt. The visible apparition is both the most frightening and rarest kind of spirit. They may be the rarest because it may take a lot of energy to project a visible image. As time goes by ghosts generally fade away and may only be heard. They may act only on the anniversary of their creation. Even the noises fade over time, until nothing is left of the ghost.

Other ghosts seem able to recharge themselves. Cold spots, light bulbs dimming and electronic machinery going haywire or drained batteries may be the result of spirits gathering energy from around them. These cold spots are sometimes accompanied by erratic magnetic fields. Some people have suggested that these cold spots are actually doorways between a spiritual dimension and our own.

Another possible theory is that all ghostly phenomena is created by energies of living people. One part of this theory is that ghosts do exist and they gather the energy to manifest themselves from their environment. They convert heat from a room into energy; accounting for sudden drops in temperature. This can also include the energy from living people. The study of ghosts is only a small part of parapsychology. Far more money and time is spent researching the powers of the human mind. Just as the mind can create psychosomatic illnesses in the body, it may be able to create a ghost as a symptom of its beliefs or fears. Researchers speculate that some people who have seen ghosts are actually psychic and that they have read the mind of people, and convinced themselves that the information came from supernatural sources.

Still other people have speculated that some forms of mediumship like the Ouiji board and crystal gazing are forms of hypnosis. The person doing the "scrying" or receiving visions is not psychic or under the influence of a spirit. They are actually using their subconscious abilities to pick up cues from their own memories and audience in a self-induced trance. There was a case where people created their own ghost as an experiment. In the early 1970s a group of paranormal investigators from Toronto, Canada experimented with psychic energies and created a ghost. They felt that it might be possible to create the illusion of a persona in their own minds and see if paranormal phenomena or a haunting would result. After several weeks of concentrating on their ghost, they were successful. This has of course come under a skeptical view that disputes the reality of these experiments and other ghostly phenomenon.

A skeptic is a person who looks at paranormal phenomenon and tries to find an ordinary, scientific explanation what happened. To do this, skeptics prefer to visit haunted sites themselves and investigate them, question witnesses and propose scientific and reasonable explanations for what has happened. People who are devout believers in the spirit world find themselves at odds with the skeptics at times. From my experience the skeptic is just as imaginative and wants to believe in ghosts as much as the "True-Believer", they just need a little bit more convincing. Just look at the amount of time and money and effort they spend investigating hauntings.

Parapsychology research has led to theories that some hauntings and "ghosts" are actually caused by sound waves. Certain sounds can have strange physiological effects on the human body, including causing anxiety, fear and even hallucinations. Other sounds were thought to have been so soothing and extra-earthly that they could summon spirits and angels. Skeptics now of course dispute this belief. While they can find rational and correct explanations for some alleged hauntings, some skeptics can come up with some highly detailed, unlikely, even improbable chains of coincidence when they try to rationalize or explain the paranormal. Sometimes it would be more likely to be struck by lightning, or a ghost.

The English philosopher William of Ockham, who died in 1349, coined a phrase that I like to use when looking at paranormal phenomena. He said (and I quote), "*pluralites non est ponenda sine necessitate*" for those readers who do not speak Latin, this roughly means; *when trying to solve a problem with several different explanations; the simplest answer is probably the correct one.* It's also called Ockham's Razor, because it cuts through elaborate explanations to the heart of the matter.

I have included a section called *Some Thoughts on Ghosts and Ghost Hunting* at the end of this book. In this section I examine some of the natural phenomenon that has been mistaken for hauntings in the past. This can range from wet plaster, to subsonic vibrations to self-hypnosis. I also discuss some of the newest tools in ghost hunting and some interesting historic perspectives on ghosts, like the Armonica. Whether you are a skeptic or a believer, you may find this of interest.

Native American Spirits and Sacred Places

In the past, dedicated but misguided missionaries and pioneers disturbed many Native American spiritual sites. Many have been destroyed, buried by development or under water behind dams. The Native American inhabitants of this region have many different religious traditions. They have developed different religious and cultural traditions based upon their environment, experiences and contact with other peoples. Within Washington and Oregon there are Indian Tribes who speak dozens of dialects of languages such as Chinookan, Sahaptain and Salish. Many groups were isolated from each other by natural barriers like mountains and cultural barriers like language and custom. What might be a "normal" belief in one village or tribe might still be observed to a greater or lesser extent by any given individual.

In mythological times, the earth was inhabited by many different beings. Almost all of these beings had supernatural powers that were used for good or evil, depending upon the nature of the being. One of these beings, the Great Spirit, had many names; the Chinooks called him *Talipus* and the Klikitats; *Spilyai.*

Spilyai was immortal. He was famous for his various adventures and pranks. He was described as having the head of an old man with frizzy hair and the body of a prairie wolf. If his body were destroyed, it would be restored to life and form in time. He turned all of the *Skookums* or demons into stones and animals. *Scotam* was a powerful female chief who lived in mythological lands west of Puget Sound. She was full of mischief and brought diseases like smallpox to the Native Americans.

Next in power below the divine beings are the *Skookums* or *Elip Tillicum,* the demons. The generic name of *Skookum* from the Chinook means sturdy or powerful. *Elip Tillicum* were often dangerous or sought to hurt human beings. Although they were not gods, like *Spilyai*, they were more common and so more likely to affect the lives of the average every day Native American. *Spilyai* destroyed most of the *Elip Tillicum* in the past.

Most of them were turned into inanimate objects like trees or rocks. In some cases they kept some of their old powers. Others kept their old forms but had reduced power. There are many historic maps of the Pacific Northwest that have *Skookum Meadows* or *Skookum Hills* drawn on them. That was why it was important for hunters to leave offering to the resident spirits in some of these places. Or when they were travelling in unfamiliar territory. You never knew when you might be standing next to an old demon, able to harm you if you did not properly thank it for its help in your hunting and gathering.

Native Americans and most aboriginal people living around the world have considered mountains and other high places sacred. There is a great debate as to why this is true. Mountains are landmarks. They can define territory. Mountains are hard to climb; it takes effort and courage to get to the top. This alone could be the reason they are sacred. When you are at the top, you can see for miles around. This can lend itself to a clearer vision particularly if someone climbed the mountain to seek personal or spiritual insight. If you believe that heaven is in the sky, mountains are closer to Heaven. What about strange phenomena?

Some strange but natural things can happen on mountains. Most mountains are the result of volcanic action, particularly high peaks like Mt. Adams, Mt. Hood, Mt. Ranier and Mt. St Helen's. A volcanic eruption is proof even to modern people of the existence of God. Particularly if you are nearby when it happens. If you make it to the top of very high mountains the oxygen becomes thin. If you exert yourself you can experience oxygen deprivation and its effects. The effects range from confusion to a slowing of mental understanding and possibly hallucinations. All of these have at one time or another been attributed to spiritual factors. Stranger things can happen in the mountains.

There is a natural phenomenon called ball lightning. This begins deep in the earth's crust. Tectonic plates rub against each other prior to or after an earthquake. When this happens, static electricity is generated. This is similar to rubbing your hand against a cat's fur. The friction of your hand against the cat generates static electricity, which is released as sparks. In ball lightning the sparks are much larger. They are released along the fault line on the surface. It makes sense that over time people living or travelling through the mountains will witness this and spread the story. A story like that would tend to remain in a people's memory for a long time.

Part of the spiritual life of the Indian youths was to go on a vision quest. Many of the sacred places were high up in the mountains. Humanity as a whole has always venerated high places, perhaps for their isolation. Boys approaching manhood would go into the mountains or other sacred places where the spirits were close. The aim of the young boys was to see visions of the past or future and a spirit guide who would give them power for the rest of their lives.

The youths would not eat and would stay awake at night without a blanket. Sometimes the visions would come easily. For others who were less sensitive (hardheaded?) the visions would not come. The boys would usually engage in heavy physical work to weaken their bodies and allow the spirits to show themselves. To do this, they frequently piled large rocks into walls or mounds. They would do this many times until exhaustion made them collapse and brought on visions. In extreme circumstances they might cut a digit from a finger or toe which would bring on shock and visions. In some tribes people ate or smoked certain herbs to bring on the visions. It is unusual but among the Chinook, some women would also go on a vision quest.

Silver Star Mt. (Skamania County, Washington)

A well known system of pits and rock piles exist on the ridge south of Silver Star Mountain, just east of the Clark County/Skamania County line in southern Washington. At least 26 pits, trenches and rock piles have been mapped by in recent years. There are several different explanations for these pits. Pioneers used to call them the "rifle pits".

There is a story about a group of soldiers who were traveling from the Vancouver Barracks to Ft Simcoe in Eastern Washington. They were ambushed and trapped on Silver Star Mt. For defense they excavated several pits and built low rock walls to protect themselves from the Native Americans. After a day or two they were able to slip away and return to the Vancouver Barracks. I have visited the pits several times. It would have taken quite some time to make them.

Pioneer stories tell of Native Americans using the pits and trenches as hunting blinds. They would wait in the pits for game being driven uphill by other hunters. It is possible that pits were dug and rocks were piled as rituals for a vision quest. A better location for a vision quest would have been on the top of the mountain. Unfortunately, the US Forest Service cleared and constructed a fire lookout on top of Silver Star MT many years ago. This destroyed any rock piles or cairns; so we will never know. There is no telling how many hilltops had burial grounds in the Cascade Mountains that have been accidentally destroyed or hidden by modern road and construction activities.

In 1992 I worked for the Gifford Pinchot National Forest. I hiked up to Silver Star Mountain several times. The pits are located about a half mile past the peak. On one visit I was working at the pits. I had been expecting my boss to arrive and help me. Several times I heard his voice. I would hear a few words and then silence. Each time I looked up there was no one there. I finished my work and left. It found out later that he was at the top of Silver Star Mountain, a half mile away from the pits with the film crew of PBS's *Oregon Field Guide*. They spent several hours walking over the peak, filming an episode for the show. The only explanation that we had was that his voice had been carried a half mile by the strong winds that always blow across Silver Star.

A Family Reunion? (an unnamed campground along the Cowlitz River)

Although Angela LaEre lives in the Dakotas, she was born in Washington and still returns when she can. Angela is the granddaughter of one of the last full-blooded Cowlitz Indians. One of her regrets is that she never had a chance to meet him, because he died before she was born.

In 1998 one of the burial grounds used by the Cowlitz Indian tribe was turned into a campground. Following Washington's State laws, descendents of the people buried at the cemetery were consulted and the bodies were removed and reburied in a respectful manner. At the grand opening of the campground Angela's mother, Mae and her aunts were given a grand tour. During the tour her mother took several pictures. The tour stopped at the site of the burial ground. It was an emotionally charged moment for Mae and her sisters. There was a lone tree that had grown in a strangely twisted shape. Mae spent a few minutes looking at the tree before taking a picture. She wanted to find just the right camera angle.

When the roll of film was developed they all received a shock. None of the photographs had turned out, except for the picture of the tree in the burial ground. When they looked closely at the tree they could see a wispy, smoky figure standing in front of the tree. They discussed the figure, trying to find a reasonable explanation for it and the ruined exposures. They remembered that there had not been any campfires burning nearby. The camera itself worked fine, both before and after that one roll of film. Was there a problem with the film or the exposure setting on the camera? If so, it is an interesting coincidence that the only picture that turned out was the one taken of the most emotionally charged spot in the campground.

Angela has the picture now. She will be visiting her grandfather's original grave site this October. She intends to take another picture of the same tree. She hopes that she may get a chance to meet or see him.

A Shaman's work is...(Unspecified location near Ellensburg, WA)

Being a Native American Shaman in our times is not an easy thing. Red Elk is a shaman who deals with both Native American's and Euro Americans in Eastern Washington. Many shamans, mediums or priests, regardless of their religion have to deal with many people with many problems. In some cases the shaman may have to refer a patient to the "White Man's" medicine, as in the case of a broken arm or leg. In other cases, they have to deal with supernatural events like haunted houses, spirit attacks or some "cultural" illnesses many Native Americans (or Euro-Americans) suffer trying to fit into our modern world. This requires the shaman to be a combination psychologist, philosopher, family counselor and friend to his or her patients.

Some people have confronted Red Elk because they think that he is a sorcerer. A shaman is a man or woman who is able to commune with supernatural beings or channel supernatural energies to perform exorcisms. For want of a better word, magic. A sorcerer is a shaman who uses his or her power for selfish or evil reasons. Red Elk is careful to use his powers for good and will not do anything that he deems hurtful to any living or dead person.

He believes that ghosts are very much alive. When people see or confront a ghost they are in reality slipping backward in time to see the ghost or the ghost has slipped forward in time to see them. Most people in our present do not know how to control this slip, which is why it is accidental for them. Ghosts do know how to control the time slip so it is intentional on their part, like one he encountered in the January of 1999.

Red Elk was contacted by representatives of the Yakamas Indian Tribe. They asked him to go with one of their holy men and an archaeologist to look at land that might have been an old burial ground. Once they identified the burial site, they would protect it from a future development. Over the years, particularly the last 50 years, the locations of many remote traditional cemeteries have been forgotten. Despite the cold weather, he agreed. They visited the location.

It was a sunny cold afternoon when they arrived at the site. Red Elk told them to stay in the vehicle and he would look at the site. He wanted some privacy so he could pray and see if there were any Indian spirits on the site. He left his car and began walking across the open field. He had to take cautious little steps to avoid slipping and falling on the ice, which was several inches thick. When he reached the middle of the field he stopped and prayed over the frozen ground. While he was doing this, the Yakamas representative and their archaeologist left their car and walked up behind him.

After a few minutes of prayer Red Elk watched as the solid figure of a Native American brave rose, head first out of the ice about 30 feet away. The man was about 40 years old, which marked him as an "older" man in prehistoric terms. The spirit did not say anything, but he pointed to a spot a few feet away. Red Elk understood. This was where the man and 30 or 31 other people were buried. Red Elk then spoke with the spirit and told him that they would return and perform a ceremony for the dead. The spirit nodded its head and slowly slipped into the ground, feet first. Red Elk spoke to his companions without turning his head.

"Did you sense anything strange", he asked?

There was no reply. He repeated his question. Again he was answered by silence. He finally turned his head. He watched his companions running across the slick ice toward their vehicle. The archaeologist, who was in his mid-50s was running so hard that his knees were rising up, almost hitting him in the chest. The Yakamas was more dignified and refused to run; but he took some very long, quick steps across the ice.

"Well, did you sense anything?" Red Elk yelled to them. This time he got a reply.

"Yes we did", came the reply. The two men had reached their vehicle, entered, locked the doors and rolled up the windows by the time Red Elk reached them. They would not tell him exactly what they sensed or saw. They also declined his invitation to come back with him and pray over the location the spirit had pointed to. Next time they will listen to Red Elk.

Eagle to Shaman

Ghostly Shaman of Glenacres Golf Course, (1000 S 112th, Seattle, WA)

This is story began as a story of a case of indecent exposure. In the early 1960s people playing golf on the Glenacres golf course in Seattle were surprised to see a naked man dancing around the golf course.

In the spirit of propriety, especially at a private golf club the police were called to remove the interloper. They approached a thin, almost gaunt man whirling and ducking in elaborate circles. When they closed in on him, he vanished. This has happened on several occasions. Other details were added by subsequent investigations. Although the man moved with great energy and appeared to be chanting or singing, no one has ever heard the sound of his voice. Sometimes he has been seen dancing while hovering above the ground.

Reports still come in from time to time. Is this the spirit of a shaman, still praying over an old burial ground, or did stories of an Indian graveyard explain his presence? Graveyard guardians frequently appear after their resting places are disturbed. Were there modifications to the grounds in the 1960s that awakened a sleeping spirit? Does he dance on a hilltop that is no longer there; bulldozed by recent landscaping?

Chief Umtuch

The city of Battle Ground was settled in 1862. It was named for a battle that never took place seven years before. The 1850s were a troubling time for American settlers in Clark and Skamania Counties. Many Native Americans began to realize how large the United States settlement in their land was becoming. They struck out in many locations in defense of their property rights. In 1855 a group of Native Americans from Cathlapootle (near modern Ridgefield), were taken to the Vancouver Barracks. They were afraid that they were going to be killed or sent away and some escaped.

Cavalry Troop leader Captain Strong and a detail of 30 men pursued them. They met between Bells' Mountain and present day Battle Ground. Strong persuaded their leader, Chief Umtuch (or Umtux), to return to the Barracks. Umtuch returned to his people to begin the process of gathering them together for a return to the Vancouver Barracks. Shortly afterward shots rang out and Chief Umtuch was found dead by a party of soldiers. Captain Strong reported that he thought other Native Americans had killed Umtuch. Strong collected statements to support this.

The Native Americans who were there pointed out there were several bullet holes in their Chief's body. This suggested to them and others that Umtuch had been assassinated. They did not know who was behind the conspiracy, but they swore none of them had killed their Chief. Strangely enough after the long Army pursuit, the Native Americans were granted a parole of four days to bury his body and return to the Barracks. This forestalled a true battle at Battle Ground. Does Chief Umtuch still ride his pony around Chelatchie Prairie at night in search of his assassins.

One possible resting place for Chief Umtuch is Tum Tum

Mountain

Tum Tum Mountain, (Chelatchie Prairie, Washington)

Old timers who lived in Chelatchie Prairie used to talk about lights like fire beacons on the top of the mountain on autumn nights. Sometimes people have also heard voices chanting on these and other nights. Are the rituals for the dead still being performed? There were, and are several different groups of Native Americans in the Pacific Northwest. They were all highly mobile, traveling along trails through the hills and mountains. Part of the way this network of travel and trade was maintained was because nearly everyone spoke a kind of universal trade language that was a mix of the local languages, English and French. It was called the Chinook Jargon. Before Euro-American settlement in the Pacific Northwest there were over a million people who spoke the Chinook Jargon.

In the Chinook Jargon, there are different ways to translate the name Tum Tum. *Tum* could mean *spirit*, or *heart* or *sacred.* I prefer to think that the repeated name Tum Tum means something like, *Sacred Heart* Mountain. People visiting the wide-open Chelatchie Prairie would understand why it might be considered sacred. Tum Tum Mountain stands like a sentinel over the flat land and low hills surrounding it. In summer and fall thousands of Native Americans would have gathered to pick bracken fern roots (yes, bracken fern roots!) and huckleberries as well as race horses, renew family ties and worship together. In the last few years there has been a renewed encampment every summer of Native Americans with interested people to renew this tradition.

Works Consulted

Books

Lind, Carol

1933 *Western Gothic*, Lind Publishing, Seattle.

Periodicals

Gibbs, George

1955 - 1956 "Account of Indian Mythology in Oregon and Washington Territories". *Oregon Historical Quarterly* 56 (4): 293 - 325, 57

(2)pp. 125 - 167, edited by Fila Clark.
Shroll, Marilee
1972 "Story of a Town Named For a `Non-Battle' ". *Clark County History*, Vol. 13, pp. 5-9. Fort Vancouver Historical Society of Clark County, Inc., Vancouver, WA.
Van Arsdol, Ted
1992 "Vancouver Barracks and the Indians". *Clark County History*, Vol. 33 pp. 19-25. Fort Vancouver Historical Society, of Clark County, Inc., Vancouver, WA.

The Portland Basin

Rural settlements in the United States during the late 1800s depended upon a farmer's ability to get to the store for those things he could not provide for himself. This included factory goods, farm equipment, specialty foods, mail and a large number of other items. The need to go to the store had to be balanced against the limitations of the farmer's transport; the horse or oxen drawn wagon.

The farmer had to be able to take his wagon (and family), to the store, drop off produce, pick up any goods and make it back home in the course of a single day. Depending upon terrain it could take one hour or several to travel four or five miles. This led to a series of small "one horse towns" dotting rural Washington and Oregon.

Battle Ground, Washington

The Farmer Who Wouldn't Move (Battle Ground, Washington)

Southwest Washington's green space is shrinking at a rapid rate. Today or tomorrow people may find themselves hosting a ghost that used to haunt empty range. The land between Vancouver and Battle Ground was subdivided early in this century for homesteads. During the Great Depression one of the recovery efforts of the US Government involved subdividing government lots and turning them into small farm holdings. Most of these little farms consisted of 40 or less acres of land. The farm house was usually a small shack made from anything people could find; from rough lumber to wooden crates. Many people broke their hearts and bodies trying to keep their small farms going. Gradually these family farms were sold and added to larger farm holdings or subdivided into smaller residential lots.

In the 1980s Jack and his family bought a 5-acre parcel

of land from man who had inherited 40 acres from his deceased father. When they bought the land, it was used as a horse pasture. Despite the piles of road apples and cow pies, Jack's family fell in love with their property and quickly moved a mobile home onto a level spot of ground. The family had moved in and had settled into their new home for several weeks before anything strange began to happen.

That summer was very hot. The heat kept their teenage daughter up late at night. One night as she lay in bed trying to sleep, she began to hear the creak of a rocking chair rocking on a wooden floor. This was doubly strange because she did not have a rocking chair. Furthermore, her bedroom floor was carpeted. She eventually fell asleep to the sound of the rhythmic creaking. In the morning she asked her parents if they had a rocking chair. She explained what she had heard over the night. The answer was no; no one in the house had a rocking chair.

They accepted it as a ghost and tried to ignore it. Over the next months the paranormal events became stronger. Although their daughter never saw anything, she heard and even felt things. When she was in her room she would sometimes hear footsteps either in her room or following her from her room into the hallway and bathroom. She sometimes felt as though someone was watching her. The footsteps and presence seemed confined to one portion of the house only, her end of the house. It was never overtly threatening, but it was watchful. The activity reached a peak, in a surprisingly physical way.

One evening Jack heard a screech from the bathroom. He saw his daughter running out of the bathroom wearing only a towel. She yelled that the ghost had slapped her while she was getting out of the bathtub. She showed Jack and her mother her hip, which bore the red imprint of a large palm and five fingers. Once their daughter calmed down, she admitted that the slap had not hurt, it had just surprised her.

After this incident the spirit seemed to loose strength. Jack's daughter was never touched again. After a time, the footsteps gradually faded away. The sound of the rocking chair was the last sound that she heard, as it too faded away. Later Jack met with the former property owner and questioned him on the history of that piece of property. The man admitted that there had been a small farm shack located within the pasture. His father had lived there. The old man had built the small house and refused to leave, even when the son tried to get him to move into a bigger, better house. He felt tied to the land. The old man used to sit in his rocking chair on the front porch on summer evenings and watch the stars. Jack asked what happened to the old man. The son replied that when his father died they pulled the house down but buried him in the pasture, near thc house site.

Where exactly was the grave? The grave and house site were on the site of Jack's new house. His daughter's room was directly over the old house's front porch. How many of these other small family farms are haunted by the spirits of their former owners, sitting on their ghostly rocking chairs, waiting for the neighbors to move in?

Cornelius, Oregon

The Old Storm House (now gone, about 5 miles south of Cornelius, Oregon)

In 1937 Barbara Haas and her husband were looking for a place to live. This was at the height of the Great Depression. There were few options open to them. There were few jobs in the city. They decided it would be better to try living in the country. They found a vacant farmhouse. The nearby farmer had bought the land after the previous owners had left. He told the Haas family that he would not charge them any rent. He said they would not be staying long. Barbara and her family met the same reaction when they told their mostly German-American neighbors where they were living. Everyone knew about the Storm House.

The farm had a huge barn and a well with pump just

outside the back door of the farmhouse as well as a large shed. The previous tenants had left a rough plank table and cook stove in the kitchen. The house was surrounded by many trees, which gave it a peaceful setting. No one had broken any of the windows either. At first they did not notice anything too unusual about the house. They did feel a little uncomfortable in the front rooms where the parlor and social room were. They preferred the comfortable kitchen anyway. Barbara and her husband decided to keep to the back rooms of the house.

The summer had been warm and dry and they stayed outside most of the time. In fall they were inside more and began to notice strange things. The well and kitchen were located at the north end of the house. Barbara and others would hear the sound footsteps walking across the boards that covered up the well. The sound would echo when the footsteps crossed over the wooden planks covering the well. When Barbara stepped out the kitchen door to welcome her visitors, there was no one there.

After a few months one of their neighbors told them more about some previous owners. According to the neighbor, the previous owners, the Strums had been bootleggers. It was a profitable, but dangerous profession. They had hidden liquor in trapdoors located in many rooms of the house. The Haas's had already discovered three excavated hiding holes under the floors. In addition to the bootlegging, the Strums may have been involved in a murder. According to local stories, a man had been killed on the stairs leading from the entry hall to the living room. Barbara had noticed blood stains on the stair landing and up four or five steps. Now she knew where they had come from.

Barbara's family and their guests had heard footsteps walking up the blood stained stairs. They sounded like a man's heavy tread. They would always pause for a few minutes after reaching the stained stairs and then continue upward to the living room. The footsteps would walk into the room and halt at the trap door located there. After several minutes the footsteps would begin at the foot of the stairs again. There may have been another ghost who was shyer then the man on the stairs.

Almost every month, at the full moon the Haas's would hear the sound of bare feet walking from the kitchen floor, through the living room into the empty south bedroom where Barbara and her husband slept. The footsteps were lighter, like a woman's. Sometimes the heavier masculine ones followed the lighter footsteps. Both of them stopped when they reached the bedroom window. Was this the ghost of an unfortunate woman waiting for her lost lover? Or were a man and a woman both killed that fateful night?

Barbara and her family could not afford to move, no matter how eerie things became. Aside from an occasional fright they got along with their ghosts. They lived there for two years until their second child was born in 1939. At that time Barbara's husband found work in another location and the whole family moved to a new house. A few years later there was a massive fire that destroyed the house and barn. Was this an accident or did the nearby folk decide it was time to do away a spiritual blight?

Portland, Oregon

The Bagdad Theater (2702 SE Hawthorne, Portland)

The Bagdad Theater is one of many Arabian Knights style of theaters built in the late 1920s, after silent fantasy classics like Douglas Fairbank's *Thief of Baghdad.* There were thousands of movie theaters like this in medium and small towns across America. Many of these theaters reached out to their audiences with live Vaudeville performances as well as movies. The Bagdad Theater will comfortably seat 700 + people in its auditorium and large balcony. Several rows of seats have been removed to make way for the permanent tables, set up in front of many seats for patrons to place their food and drink while watching movies.

I spoke with managers Ed and Kevin and several employees. There were several paranormal events that happened during the renovation of the theater and its reopening. These have gradually tapered off, but odd things still happen. Patty worked at the Bagdad in 1994 when McMenamins first acquired it. She knew things would be different after the electricians began rewiring the theater. They turned off the main power switch to the house lights. At first the lights went out normally. Suddenly they came on again, then gradually flicked off and on for nearly an hour before they stayed off. The electricians were monitoring the circuit with a voltmeter and could not explain what happened. She watched the wheeled garbage cans in the kitchen move across the floor under their own power. Employees witnessed this several times.

Patty's boyfriend worked with her at the Bagdad. One day he went up to the second floor restroom used by employees. This restroom had been a dentist's office in the past. It was not his favorite restroom because it did not have any ventilation. This time he got more ventilation than he could wish for. He was washing his hands when he felt a sudden chill. Then a cold wind began to blow through the closed room. It was so strong that the toilet paper on the rolls and the cloth towel on the circular towel rack were blown sideways. He never used that bathroom after that.

Sally Anne began working at the Bagdad a few months after these events. She never had any strange experiences, but several customers who used the downstairs bathroom told her that they thought that someone or something was down there, watching them. Her roommate, who was psychic refused to go down there because of this presence. Although she never saw anything, Sally Anne and other employees who were in the kitchen would sometimes feel as if someone was watching them from the windows of the swinging doors that separated the kitchen from the lobby.

The theater was used for Vaudeville as well as movies. One night after the performances were over, the theater's janitor hung himself backstage. His body was not found until the next morning. Since then the spirit of the unhappy janitor has haunted the backstage area and basement. I spoke with several employees who work backstage. One man told me that although he hasn't seen anything strange, he sometimes scares himself when he's there alone. There are only a few low wattage lights to brighten up the high ceiling room. When I was back there I noticed a mannequin handing from the ceiling near the stairs leading to the basement. I asked about it.

"Oh," the worker replied as if seeing it for the first time. "There's been a noose hanging from the ceiling ever since this placed opened as a McMenamins. The doll is new though." Another worker confirmed this statement. No one knew who had hung the rope, but it is associated with the story of the suicidal theater manager.

The Boy of Sullivan's Gulch (The Granada Court Apartments, 23rd and NE Pacific, Portland, Oregon)

Like many large cities in the world, Portland started out as a small community that grew faster than it's neighboring villages and towns. As it grew, it gradually swallowed up its smaller neighbors. One small hamlet swallowed up by Portland was Sullivan's Gulch. Part of the early industry of Sullivan's Gulch was brick making.

In 1910 the large brick mill was razed and a large apartment complex building was constructed on its site. In the early 1990s Brenna was looking for an apartment not too far from work, but not "in" the city. She instantly fell in love with Granada Court. The apartments are a series of single story duplexes built in a vaguely hacienda style. The only thing that was not perfect was her inability to get a goodnights sleep. No matter how tired and sleepy and sleepy she was, when she lay down she would begin feeling restless, which would keep her up late.

Her pet cat, "Kitty" began acting strangely too. One of Kitty's favorite resting places was at the foot of Brenna's bed. One evening Brenna was lying in bed reading and for some reason looked up at Kitty. The cat had stopped grooming herself and was staring fixedly at a spot on the wall, or at something standing by the wall. The cat's head began to swivel, as if it was watching someone walk from that spot to the bedroom door. The cat's head tracked the invisible movement upward, as if watching something rising up to and through the ceiling. After that Kitty began grooming herself again.

On another occasion Brenna, her boyfriend and (again) Kitty were in her bedroom. The light was on and Brenna and her boyfriend were talking. Without warning all of them heard a child's voice loudly exclaiming, "*OOOOH*!" as if in surprise or amusement. The sound seemed to come from the middle of her open bedroom doorway at a height of about 4 feet. All of them, Kitty included turned to face the sound when it happened.

Like many older apartments Brenna's had some odd construction quirks. Her bedroom door opened into a cul-de-sac with three other doors at the end of a hallway. After this initial incident, Brenna and some of her guests would periodically hear the childish exclamations at odd hours at the end of the hallway. She never mentioned the sound, but would wait for her guests to react. Although some left in fear, it never bothered Brenna. After a while Brenna began to echo the voice with a whistle, because her voice could not reach such a high pitch.

Brenna lived in her apartment for over three years. During that time the haunting increased in intensity. Brenna's cat, Kitty died and was replaced by a new one she named

Merlin. Merlin used to watch invisible people move around the apartment just as Kitty used to do. Merlin also seemed to hear the child's voice. Brenna moved her bed into the apartment's smaller bedroom and later to her living room in search of a good night's sleep.

She noticed that a small light about the size of a marble would appear in the little cul-de-sac hallway. It seemed to float across the little hallway at a height of about four feet, the same as the voice. Sometimes it would move to one of the closed doors and disappear.

Brenna's friends moved into the next door apartment. After a short time they mentioned the fact that they were not sleeping well. Their bedroom was next to Brenna's haunted bedroom. They also mentioned seeing a floating light that seemed to appear from the wall of their apartment where it joined with hers. She had not mentioned the light to them before that time. They exchanged experiences.

Another friend brought over a Ouiji board and Brenna took notes. Like many Ouiji board sessions, not a lot of information came out of this first session. Some of it only made sense later. The first thing they asked was for the identity of the child. After many questions the board answered that the voice was that of a boy. His initials may have been either S.A. or A.S. He had been six years old when he died. He had lived in the apartments many years before. When asked why he stayed on, the boy/board replied that it was fun and spelled the word WHISTLE. Brenna had never mentioned whistling back at the voice to her friends on the Ouija board before. He gave clues about other spirits in the vicinity.

According to the board, there was another spirit in the area. Some time in the past a black woman had been killed in a nearby field. The information was only fragmentary and they could not get more specific answers as to dates and names. It was enough for Brenna and her friends. They were all shaken and did not try to contact the spirits again.

A year later Brenna had a frightening series of dreams.

She dreamt that she was being held down by something that was invisible. She was able to turn her head and looked beside her bed. She saw a black woman wearing a black dress with a white design sewn or embroidered on it. The woman looked very angry. Brenna could not get up or breathe for several seconds. After several seconds she would be able to slowly rise. She could also feel her mother's presence nearby. Finally Brenna was able to sit up in bed. At that point she would wake up and find that the whole paralysis episode had been a dream. This was repeated three times.

On the fourth and last time she had the dream it ended differently. It began like the rest. Brenna felt herself being held down. She saw the woman. Brenna got out of bed slowly. This time she ran out of her bedroom and turned on all of the lights in her apartment. She turned on the kitchen faucet and splashed her face with water. She realized that this time she was awake. She did not go back to bed that night.

Was Brenna suffering from sleep paralysis brought on by her sleep deprivation? One of the symptoms of this natural phenomenon is the feeling that someone is holding you down and the feeling of a weight on your chest. Could the Ouiji board session have planted the suggestion or an image of the black woman in Brenna's subconscious where it waited a year or so to materialize? Or was this a visitation by the ghost of an angry spirit who formed a connection to Brenna during the séance? After three years of living in northeast Portland, Brenna had an opportunity to move to England, which she took. She regretted leaving Merlin behind but she does not miss the little boy, the black woman or her insomnia.

Carlos Still Lives at Mohawk Street (Portland, Oregon)

In 1990 Ed and Tom, a father and son bought a fixer upper house. The seller had included an as-is clause in the sale contract. Since both father and son enjoyed doing carpentry they were not concerned about structural problems. They did want to find out any specific areas that needed special work.

The house was large, with a finished basement and two stories. All the seller would say was that his family would never enter the house again.

This may have given them pause for thought, but they were not worried. They began major renovations to the interior of the house. After a few months the ghostly activities began. Ed and Tom began to hear footsteps pacing the hallways. The cassette player would also be shut off when unseen hands pushed the eject button. When Tom was working in the basement or in the first floor hallway he would often be touched or tapped by an invisible hand. On other occasions while he was climbing the basement stairs Tom has had someone shout "Hey Now!" in his ear. Sometimes it would call "Hey You!"

His father, Ed was not immune to ghostly attentions. He had also been touched and had his hair messed by unseen hands. He too has seen a white mist that he thinks is their ghost; called Carlos. This has happened several times, usually in the main hallway. On one occasion the vapor appeared against a bedroom wall. At first it expanded to cover nearly the entire wall and then contracted until it was only a few inches wide and then disappeared. Tom has also seen the "Carlos" mist in the hallway.

Ed and Tom have been startled and irritated by Carlos, but seldom frightened except for that one time. Tom had been in the living room and heard Carlos pacing in the hallway. He wanted to call his father to listen to the noise, since Carlos usually manifested himself when Tom was there alone. In order to get Ed, Tom had to cross through the main hallway (through the Carlos mist), to get Ed who was outside. Tom did so, to no purpose. By the time the two of them returned the noise had stopped.

Ed and Tom don't know who Carlos really is or rather was. He continues to share the house with them, showing himself from time to time as if to let them know he's still around.

This story is adapted from information contained in the

web site; Ghosts of North Portland by H Michael Bell at http://www.hevanet.com/heherb.htm

Cornelius Roadhouse (4045 NW Cornelius Pass Rd, Hillsborough, Oregon)

When I approached Tim Hills of McMenamins about visiting the various haunted properties the company owns he assured me that one of the hot spots of activity was the Cornelius Roadhouse. When I arrived there, this seemed to be the case. There are several pictures painted on the walls detailing a story of tragedy in the house.

At the top of the stairs leading to the attic there is a painting of a little girl who pushed her little brother down the stairs, accidentally killing him. Her parents stand in a portrait above the fireplace on the second floor. And why does a young woman with sad eyes hide in the closet to the right of the fireplace? I found out that these events may not have taken place at all. These paintings were all done after the Imbrie family sold the building to McMenamins. They were inspired in part by some stories told to the artist. They were also painted to add to the mystique surrounding the house. I spoke with a member of the Imbrie family who informed me that the house was not haunted. Despite this, there are true stories of the strange events at the

Cornelius roadhouse.

In 1994 the third floor attic space was designated off-limits and is now kept locked. Prior to that, one of the managers had gone into the attic to store some boxes and found a circle of candles laid out on the floor with a dead bird laying in the center of the circle. Thrill seekers had been sneaking in and conducting seances at night. Whether the bird was a sacrifice or had somehow been trapped in the attic and died did not matter. They managers wanted nothing to do with either.

Several employees have experienced cold spots around the house. One spot is located on the stairs. There are other cold spots on the stair landings and near the coffee machine. Some of these can be explained by a natural draft of cold air. But why does the draft remain in the summer when the outside air is warmer than inside the house? Glasses sitting at an empty table have shattered when no one was around and footsteps have been heard walking up the stairs when the building has been closed and only the cleaning staff were present.

Christopher, the manager of the Cornelius Roadhouse originally trained as an engineer. He tries to take a logical view of the hauntings. He is quick to point out rational explanations for some of the things that he and other people have experienced. He admits that there may be no truth to the stories behind the paintings, but the house is 150 years old. That is plenty of time for several tragedies, joys, births and deaths to have filled the building with ghosts and shades.

On many occasions Christopher has been responsible for closing the building for the night. Each time he makes sure that kitchen appliances like the stoves and coffeepots are turned off. He also ensures that no one is left in the building; all of the windows are locked and the lights are turned off. His last duty is to turn on the burglar alarm and lock the front door. On two occasions after doing this he has paused at his car and looked back at the Roadhouse. On these two occasions he has seen all of the lights were now turned on. The rational explanation he proposed is that the wiring in the house is old and the lights somehow turned themselves on all by themselves.

On these occasions he did not open the building in the morning. It seems likely that they had been turned off by morning, otherwise the manager would have spoken with him about it. I do not think that this can be blamed on faulty wiring. I asked him if he had gone back into the building to investigate the wiring. Had the light switches been turned on? He laughed loudly and replied,

"I don't know. I didn't go back in!"

The Crystal Ballroom (1332 West Burnside, Portland, Oregon)

Tim Hills, historian of McMenamins has written *The Many Lives of the Crystal Ballroom.* The Crystal Ballroom is located at the corner of NW 14th and Burnside. People may notice that the corner where the streets meet is not a true 90 degree angle. In 1873 John Couch subdivided his property into parcels and oriented his parcel with the Willamette River, rather than with the streets of city of Portland. When the roads joining Portland with Couch's property were built, there was a jog where they met. This affected the design and the acoustics of the Crystal Ballroom when it was built nearly 40 years later.

At the turn of the century Montrose Ringler had become famous for his skill as a dance instructor. He had a large clientele of people from the upper classes whom he taught various modern and classical dances. Most of them refused to come to Ringler's school, which was located in a less than savory part of town. In 1913 Ringler approached Paul Van Fridagh with a proposal to build a large dance hall, music school and society center on Van Fridagh's property. It was a risky venture.

In 1913 Lola Baldwin, a local woman's suffragette and reformer, opposed dancing and dance halls. This view was based on the belief that modern dances like Jazz, liquor and saloons only led to immoral conduct. Baldwin and her coalition were so successful that the City of Portland initiated a temperance ordinance three years before Prohibition became

Clowns look down from the walls of the ballroom

legal nationwide. They also spurred the city to pass four anti-dance ordinances and hire regulators to modern the dance halls located within Portland.

Despite the opposition, Ringler convinced Van Fridagh to back his plan. In January of 1924 Cotillion Hall as the Crystal Ballroom was then known opened for business. A major attraction of the dancehall was the floating floor. It was made with a layer of fine maple planks laid on top of a series of wooden rocker panels with ball bearings attached to the ends of the rockers. This added a gentle swaying motion to the whole floor when people danced. The rocking motion could be adjusted by a series of ratchet gears to enhance the floating motion for several different dances. The Crystal Ballrooms floor may be the only one of this kind left in the United States.

In 1921 Ringler sold his lease to the Cotillion Hall, which fell under less inspired management. After the death of Paul Van Fridagh in 1925, building maintenance was not a priority and it gradually fell into disrepair. The building was renamed the Crystal Ballroom in 1950. Unfortunately, with the construction of large auditoriums like the Coliseum, the old hall could not compete for popular bands. One of the effects of the lopsided square shaped building is that there are several dead spots where patrons have a hard time hearing the band play. The Crystal Ballroom closed as a music venue in 1968 and was not reopened until 1997 when McMenamins purchased the facility and brought it back to life. At least parts of it.

Ed Lawrence is the manager of the Crystal Ballroom. In 1998 he and another employee were working late in the staff offices, one floor down from the dance floor. He was looking through a file drawer located near the open doorway. He glanced up at a noise outside the room and saw a man walk by him, heading toward his office. Ed took one step to his left, outside the doorway to investigate. It was very late and there was not supposed to be anyone in the building. The hallway was empty. The hallway was perhaps 12 feet long and ended at three offices and an exit door, all were closed and locked. Ed walked down the hallway and checked the offices to make sure they were locked and empty. They were.

Ed's co-worker had seen Ed look up, walk into the hallway and then return a moment later looking puzzled. Puzzled and very pale. Ed explained what had happened. This man had not seen the figure, but he trusted Ed's word. They both left early that night.

Christmas Eve of 1998 was not a good night for Ed either. He was entertaining company at his house when he received a call from the Crystal Ballroom's Security Company. The burglar alarms had gone off. Ed had to drive through the snow to check out the building. He walked up to the second floor, where the stairs lead to the main entrance to the ballroom. Ed wanted to surprise any intruders so he did not turn on the lights. He walked through the management offices where he got a flashlight and up the performer's stairwell. He quietly let himself into the ballroom through smaller door. There was no one there. He walked through the ballroom and then headed down the main stairs to the second floor.

He paused at the foot of the stairs, searching his pockets for his keys. He wanted to open the doors to his offices. Suddenly he heard the voices of at least seven people talking very loudly at the top of the stairs leading above him. He heard their footsteps and voices grow fainter as they walked away, across the ballroom. This time Ed did not feel like investigating. He believes that even in the dark, there is no way that many people could have followed him across the entire length of the dance floor without his hearing them. Having walked across the creaking, floating floor I would agree. Whether they were ghosts or thrill seekers, there were too many of them for Ed's tastes. He left. The next morning he checked the building and found everything in its place.

I spoke with several of the other employees. More than one person has been in the ballroom after hours and heard the sound of someone walking across the floating floor. Another man was sitting in the Mezzanine when he heard the sound of someone dropping a heavy book or box on the ballroom floor. Again, there was no one there. The elevator seems to have a mind of it's own. After a show it can take several hours to break down the stage. The band's roadies and Ballroom employees are usually packing things up until 3:00 AM. This can take several trips down the elevator with the equipment. There have been several occasions when the movers have unloaded the elevator only to watch it close its doors and travel up the third floor. More often than not, they have all been down on the first floor, cursing the faulty elevator or the ghost.

Perhaps it is the Crystal Ballrooms association with music has made ghost sounds common. During the winter of 1998, one of the assistant managers was using the men's room on the second floor. It was quiet at the Ballroom, which was empty. He thought there was a party at Ringler's Annex, located directly below the restroom. Sometimes sounds from the Annex carry up to the second floor. He was drying his hands when he heard what sounded like people talking and laughing in the pub below.

He went downstairs, perhaps to join the party. He walked into a very quiet Ringler's Annex. There were only a few customers nursing their drinks. He could clearly hear music playing over the stereo system. After a quick question to the bartender to verify there had been no party a few minutes prior, he returned to his office shaking his head. Was there a party in the past that had somehow been trapped in the walls and pipes of the building waiting for a quiet night to finally echo away? Or was it just his imagination?

The Kennedy School (5736 NE 33rd, Portland, OR)

In 1913 John D Kennedy donated a large parcel of rural

farmland near of the Portland City limits (at that time 42nd Avenue) for a school. He hoped that a new school would lead to an increase in development in the area, which would improve his own real estate business. More importantly, his children needed to go to school and there was not a decent one nearby. It was not by chance that he donated land adjacent to his own house.

The Kennedy school started out as a series of portable buildings with very few amenities. The real school building was completed in 1916. The school was designed along the lines of a classic Italian villa, with several protected courtyards where the children could play. Architect Floyd Naramore incorporated several designs that were years ahead of their time. The school was designed with only a single story, so that children would not be trapped on a second story or stairwell by a fire. Additions to the school were also cheaper because they only needed to build a single story at a time. In keeping with the Italian style design, Kennedy donated a large classical style frieze that still hangs at the entrance to the school.

Unfortunately for the student body and administration, enrollment in the school district declined during the 1970s. The school administration decided the Kennedy school was too expensive to maintain and it was shut down in 1980. The school was vacant for nearly 17 years. In that time it was the haunt of vandals and drug dealers until it was taken over and renovated by the McMenamins who turned into a restaurant and Bed and Breakfast.

I visited the Kennedy School in April of 1999 without much hope of hearing any stories of hauntings there. I had spoken earlier with Liz, the manager. She told me that she did not know of any ghosts at the Kennedy school. However, she had worked at the Edgefield when it was first opened and had quite a few stories from there. So I drove to the Kennedy School and waited in the restaurant for Liz to tell me of her experiences. Liz was busy that day, and had missed breakfast. She asked if I minded if she ate as we talked. I said no. I heard some very interesting stories, while narrowly avoiding being impaled on her salad fork, which she forcefully poked in my general direction when she came to the exciting parts. After several minutes of talk about the Edgefield I asked her if she was sure that there were no ghosts or ghostly stories about the Kennedy School.

She replied with a firm, "No, there are no ghosts here, otherwise I would have heard of them! Isn't that right?" She asked our server.

"Actually, now that you mention it, I have had some strange experiences here," our server replied. Liz put down her fork and we both listened.

One afternoon in 1998 she was taking her break. She went into the restroom in the main building near the pizza oven. She had just settled into one of the stalls when she heard the door of the stall next to her open, close and lock. This was odd because she had not heard the bathroom door opening and closing as someone entered. She looked down and under the bathroom stall partition. There was no one there. The woman got up, washed her hands and shivered with a sudden chill. She hurried out of the bathroom and has never used it again.

This story prompted Liz to remember another incident that may have been coincidence or may have been paranormal. Shortly after the Kennedy school opened as a bed and breakfast, Liz and her assistant Cheryl inspected several of the rooms to ensure that housekeeping had cleaned them properly. They paused outside of Miss Dobie's Room, named for the woman who taught there in the 1920s. Cheryl told Liz that she had never liked the room because it felt strange to her. Cheryl inserted her master key in the room's lock and tried to open it. The lock was stuck. Cheryl jiggled the key for several minutes and could not unlock the door. Liz also tried next without success. Liz had worked at the Edgefield Poorhouse several years and had similar experiences. She apologized to the ghost for offending it and said that she really liked the room. She tried the key again and the door opened.

We spoke with several other employees after lunch. According to one, shortly after the school opened a former student came to visit the old school building. This man had been a boy when a teacher committed suicide. According to the man, a female teacher had reached the age of 27 or 28 and was still unmarried. She was so despondent over her status as an "old-Maid" that she quietly entered the coat room in the Old McDonald's room and hung herself. It was several hours before a student found her body.

Lloyd Center

Portland's Lloyd Center was one of the Pacific Northwest's earliest shopping malls. It has gone through numerous revisions and renovations since it was built. What were outside shops have now become enclosed. One of the oldest portions of the mall is at the Nordstrom's.

In the evenings, after the Mall has closed, maintenance staff members have seen an extra worker. A few years ago, one of the workers died of a heart attack on the job. Shortly after the death, a worker was riding up the escalator, which is located near the Nordstrom's store. Although the mall was closed several members of the maintenance staff were cleaning about the mall. He was not surprised to look up and see a man approaching him, riding the down escalator. The worker riding up recognized the man riding down and called a greeting as they passed each other. Than he realized that the man riding the down escalator was his deceased co-worker.

He immediately turned around and looked down, but the escalator was empty. There was no one on the floor below. The man had looked solid. He was dressed in his normal work clothes and had been carrying a wrench in his hand. It was as if the ghost was still performing his duties, into the afterlife.

I have approached a few of the maintenance workers and inquired about any strange or paranormal events in the mall. They have denied any knowledge of this story. According to the person who related this story to me, all of the staff has been sworn to secrecy. If one of the maintenance staff will admit to seeing the ghost, please let me know.

Princeton Street (Portland, Oregon)

A large house on Princeton Street has a record of haunting dating back nearly a century. A travelling businessman owned this house at the turn of the century. He left his wife and young daughter behind when he took one of his frequent trips. On one of these trips his wife died. The husband stayed at home more often, but he was not alone. His daughter told him that her mother still came at night to tuck her into bed. When he questioned her about the matter, his daughter's evidence was that she could see the imprint her mother's ghost left on the bed when she sat down to tuck her in. The man sold the house and moved on but the spirit remained at the house.

An elderly lady who later lived in the house told this story and her own experiences to her family. Many nights she would hear a rocking chair squeaking, as if someone was sitting in it. Several times she got up and went to investigate the noise. When she entered the room with the rocking chair she would find the chair, empty but rocking as if someone was seated in it. As the years went by she and her family came to accept and ignore the happenings.

When she moved out other relatives moved in. Meaghan grew up in the house and kept track of some of the more unnatural happenings. At times there were a lot of people living in the four-bedroom house. When it was empty she and others would hear strange things. Meaghan recalled many instances when late at night she heard footsteps upstairs leading from the master bedroom to the bathroom and back. This usually happened when her parents were not home or in bed. Most of the time the footsteps did not go back to the bedroom.

One afternoon she heard the footsteps from her parents room to the bathroom. She knew that her father was home in bed and decided to catch him if he were the "ghost". She ran upstairs, expecting to find her father in the hallway, on his way to the bathroom. Instead the hallway was empty and she found him in bed, fast asleep. There were other footsteps and sounds from around the house. One day she heard the front door open and close and heard footsteps walking into the house. After calling a greeting and getting no answer, she went to the entry and found it empty. Her mother said that she had had the same experience many times.

When Meaghan was a teenager, she moved into a bedroom in the basement (the refuge of many a rebellious teen). It was not always a pleasant sanctuary. Three times, while she was falling asleep she was awakened by the sound of a woman screaming in her ear. She was not sure if it was a dream or not, but she never had the experience before or after sleeping there.

The present owner of the house moved in March of 1997. He was interested in the past history of the house but had no experiences of his own to recount. He did promise to say something if he did.

This story is adapted from information contained in the web site; Ghosts of North Portland by H Michael Bell at http://www.hevanet.com/heherb.htm

Mirror Mirror (Private residence on Marine Drive, Portland, OR)

Jamie and her mother moved into a two-story white house off of Marine drive in the 1980s. It was the most beautiful house the six year old Jamie had ever seen. One of the best things about the house was the spiral staircase that led from the living room to an upstairs loft overlooking the living room. Like many families in haunted houses, they began to experience strange things shortly after moving in. It began with small things at first, then reached a peak that finally drove Jamie and her mother out of the house.

Many animals are sensitive to the paranormal. Their dog, Rebel knew something was wrong. After they moved in, whenever they let the dog out, Rebel would run to the neighbor's house. They had to go next door and physically bring him home. Jamie's mother tried to leave Rebel locked in the house when they went out. When they came home, they would find him outside in the yard or over at the neighbors. In addition to whatever was inside the house letting the dog out, there seemed to be something outside trying to get in.

Shortly after moving in Jamie and her mother were sitting in their living room watching television. Jamie began to hear a loud scratching or scraping noise from the outside walls of the house. Her mother told her it was just the sound of a tree branch rubbing against the house. They tried to ignore the periodic scratching sound. A few weeks later Jamie watched her mother mow the lawn. It was then that both of them realized that there were no trees growing near the house to cause the scratching!

When they first moved in they could not open one of the windows on the first floor. They saw that the window had been nailed shut and painted over. After numerous attempts they gave up. They did not connect this with the scratching sound, even though it was on the same side of the house. One night several months later Jamie was watching television. She heard a loud banging and pounding and then a *whooshing* noise. She and her mother looked around the house for the source of the noise and discovered the sealed window was now wide open.

Despite these strange events they did not consider moving. The house was larger than anything they had lived in since Jamie had been born. She even had her own bedroom; not that she slept there very long. On the first night she slept in her new bedroom Jamie had such terrible nightmares that she slept in mother's room the rest of the time they lived there. All in all, it was a little bit odd but not really frightening until that one incident…

Jamie's mother had broken her arm and had it in a cast. She had trouble getting dressed one morning and asked Jamie to help her. Jamie went to her mother's dresser to look for some clothing. The top of the dresser was covered with various items of make-up, jewelry, a fresh cup of coffee and a large, heavy mirror. Jamie reached out and opened the top dresser drawer, got out some clothing and shut it. The mirror seemed to jump off of the dresser top and fell toward her. Jamie's mother screamed and reached out with her good arm and pulled Jamie onto the bed as the mirror crashed to the floor.

After a few seconds they got up from the bed and looked at the mess on the floor. They walked around the glass to survey the damage to the dresser and things that had been piled on it. They were amazed to find that nothing on the dresser was out of place or damaged. Everything was in its place, including the cup of coffee. Not a drop of coffee had been spilled on the dresser. That was the final straw. They decided it was time to move.

It is a little unusual, but not eerie to find windows nailed shut in older houses. The neighborhood around Marine Drive is a little rough and a past tenant may have sealed it to keep away prowlers. If that is true, why not the other windows? As to how the window opened up on it's own, I cannot think of a simple, natural reason. The falling mirror might be explained as a natural event, but if that is so, it would be reasonable to assume that the same movement that caused the mirror to unbalance would have spilled the coffee. If the mirror fell over rather than being thrown by paranormal means, it would be expected that the things on the dresser top would have been moved or crushed by the falling mirror.

Sears Hall US Army Reserve Center (2731 Multnomah Blvd, Portland, OR)

Sears Hall, US Army Reserve Center was built in November of 1960 and dedicated in 1961. It was named after Jerome Sears, an Oregon Native who was killed in the Korean War. Sears was a student at the University of Portland, one of three students who died in the fighting. His name is inscribed on the Standing Cross War Memorial, on the University campus. Sears gave his life defending a small party of retreating comrades. In keeping with military custom, the US Army dedicated a building to his memory. It is fitting that they built Sears Hall on the same site where he used to play when he was a child.

Most of the soldiers in the Army Reserves work at their barracks one weekend a month and two weeks a year. During the rest of the month there is a tremendous amount of work that needs to be done to plan for the next drill. Because Army Reserve units can and have been activated with a a moments notice, there are a small number of full time employees at each unit. These full timers include a mix of soldiers and civilian employees.

One full time soldier is supply Sergeant Jones, who told me a few of her experiences. Her supply room is located in the rear of the building, off of the Drill Hall. The Drill Hall is a large open room with concrete floor and two rows of metal wall lockers lining one wall. On more than one occasion she heard the sound of the locks on the wall lockers rattle as if someone was walking along the row of lockers and hit them to make them clang. The sound started near the main entrance and proceeded down the row of lockers to the far end of the Drill Hall. There are over one hundred lockers. The noise was so annoying that several times she has run out of her office to yell at whomever was making the noise. Each time the noise stopped when she walked into the Drill Hall.

Years ago the Drill hall was a motor pool and a large garage-type door is located at one end of the Drill Hall. This door and the normal sized door beside it open into a fenced parking lot. On another occasion Sergeant Jones heard a loud banging in the Drill Hall. She ran out of her office and saw the garage door rattling and shaking as if someone were outside banging on it. She ran the hundred or so feet across the Drill Hall to open the side door. While she was doing this, the garage door beside it continued to rattle and bang. She threw open the door and poked her head out to see who was making the racket.

The banging stopped, there was no one there. There is no way someone standing at the garage door could have run out of sight before she could have seen them. She searched the motor pool area again and did not find anyone. The garage door is a roll up type made of heavy corrugated steel. It would have taken a gale to shake it like that. There were no heavy winds that day.

The Drill Hall with it's banging wall lockers and doors

In 1996 Major Smith was helping to plan for the deployment of several teams of soldiers to various places around the world. He worked for several weeks in the training and plans offices on the second floor west wing of Sears Hall. He was approached by one of the full-timers who had worked there for several years. The full-timer, Tom asked Smith if he had experienced anything "strange". Smith asked what he meant.

Tom replied that the ghost of Jerome Sears haunted the building. The ghost was most active in the winter evenings. Especially at the end of weekend drills when everybody was active with meetings, planning and work. These were Drills when the energy seemed to hang in the air after people had left. Tom had spent many evenings working late after Drill days like this. He would hear the sound of rubber soled boots walking down the hallway, interspersed with the sound of doors slamming. Although he would always investigate, Tom never found anything unusual. Despite the story Major Smith thought it was nothing more than a story. He forgot the story in the rush of daily work.

A few months later Smith was working late. It was about 5:30 PM in the fall. Two offices were open, his at the west end and the training office next to it. Although the office door was open it was empty. Smith heard the sound of boots walking down the hallway and entering the open training office. After several minutes of silence he became curious and walked next door. The office was empty. Shaking his head, Smith returned to his office. He guessed that someone had entered, waited a few minutes and left quietly without being heard.

About 5 minutes later Smith heard the footsteps coming back down the hallway. He called out, "The training office is empty, but I'm here."

The footsteps halted. There was no reply. He smiled to himself. He thought that Tom was pretending to be a ghost as a joke. He decided to play along. A few minutes later he heard four office doors slam in quick succession. The first was closest to him, the last door slammed shut further down the long hallway. Smith stepped out of his office and looked down the hallway. He did not see anyone. He guessed that Tom was hiding in the last office.

Smith walked down one of the two stairways to the first floor and waited for Tom to come downstairs. He wanted to surprise the "ghost". He waited about five minutes and decided to go back upstairs. When he did, he looked out of the east windows at the parking lot below. He noticed that the parking lot was empty. He was impressed with the fact that Tom had hidden his car to make the trick more convincing. Smith walked back to the stairwell and hid there, still expecting Tom to come out of the room. Ten minutes passed and still no Tom.

Major Smith started to feel silly. He had work to do and his family was waiting at home, so he walked back to his office. After a few minutes he heard footsteps in the hallway again.

Smith poked his head out of his office. There was no one there. Major Smith searched the entire second floor and once again he found it was empty. It would be nearly impossible for anyone to hide in these offices. Their only furniture is a series of small military desks and office tables.

Smith walked back to his office and sat down to get back to work. As soon as he sat down he heard footsteps walking down the hallway and the sound of doors slamming. By this time he was realizing that this was not just a joke or rite of passage. He felt a presence in the building. He also noticed that his office lights as well as his computer monitor had begun to flicker. He got up and went out in the hallway again; it was empty. He paused to look out of the window at the west end of the building. He did that quite often, to watch the sunset. There was enough light to cast shadows through the window. After a few seconds he turned away to return to his office. His gaze passed over the window of the door on the office across the hall from his own.

He stopped. He looked back at the office door window again. He saw the reflected image of human silhouette in the window. The image was shadowy and backlit. He could not distinguish any features. He could tell that it was the shape of a man with a short haircut. He thought it was his own silhouette created by the setting sun behind him. He moved his head back and forth. He spotted his own shadow moving. The other shape stayed where it was. By this comparison he could tell that the other reflection was several inches below his own. He tried to estimate where the reflection originated. He traced it back to a chair, placed in front of the west window.

Smith looked at the chair. It was a standard gray metal military chair. There was no one sitting on it. He reached out to touch the back of the chair. He did not feel anything like resistance or extreme cold, but he did experience something strange. When he reached out, the hair on his arm, beginning with the back of his hand, then wrist, then forearm raised up as if it were in contact with static electricity. He quickly pulled his hand away. The hair laid down again. He put out his arm again and again the same thing happened. He looked back at the office window. The figure was still reflected there. It had not moved.

He cleared his throat and said, "Jerome, I'm getting ready to leave, you take care of the building." He returned to his office, shut down his computer and left as quickly as possible.

When Major Smith told me this story he was very calm and composed. I could tell that it had been alarming at the time but according to Smith it was not frightening. He said that it took several minutes for the incidents to build up to this climax. This gave him time to accustom himself to the situation rather than if everything had happened at once. He did not believe the apparition or whatever it was could harm him, or was even aware of him. He had the feeling that the figure did exist in the same space as he but it was not in the same time.

I had spent a lot of time at Sears Hall before I heard Major Smith's story. I worked in the offices on the west end of the second floor for several weeks and sometimes I was the last person out of the buildings. When I came into the building in the morning Tom would ask me, "Hey Davis, did you stack these chairs in the hallway after I left?"

He would point down at one or two chairs placed along the wall outside of the office where Major Smith had seen the reflected figure. Each time I told him I had not moved the chairs he would usually snort to himself, nod his head and go into his office. I did not realize at that time why he was so curious about the chairs. Who would have come by after duty hours and gone through this ritual just to bother Tom?

To my knowledge, no one has ever died in the building. Did the dedication of this building near his childhood home bring the spirit of Jerome Sears from the battlefield of Korea to Sears Hall? Or is this haunting the result of the collected energy generated by soldiers and released as they try to compress a month of work into a two-day weekend?

Sergeant First Class Jerome F. Sears was born in 1928. In 1950 he left the University of Portland to enlist in the United States Army. He entered combat in Korea in December of 1951. By June of 1952 Sears was a veteran platoon sergeant. On the 8th of June, Sears was ordered to occupy and hold a hill in the vicinity of Sidamak, Korea. Sears led a small party of new soldiers placed on a hilltop known as Old Baldy, 200 yards outside of their lines, to act as artillery spotters. Sears voluntarily stayed with the soldiers. On the morning of the 9th of June, an intense artillery barrage hit Sears' position. Even though Sears was severely wounded he stayed at his post to encourage his fellow soldiers.

After the artillery barrage, a wave of enemy soldiers advanced on their position. Sears ordered his detachment to fall back but remained behind with another soldier, Elmer Scott. They provided covering fire against the advancing enemy. Before they could retreat, the enemy overran their position. Sears comrades regrouped and counterattacked; too late. Sears and Scott were found dead on the hilltop. For his heroism and sacrifice, Sears was posthumously awarded the Distinguished Service Cross. This is the second highest award that the US Army can give. In addition to Sears Hall in the United States, a military facility in Korea was named Camp Sears in his honor.

If you visit Sears Hall, you will find that the doors are locked. If you park in front of the building you may find your vehicle towed.

The Watchdogs at The Victorian (A private residence near 70th and SE 116th Avenue, Portland, Oregon)

Jane Cook and her son moved into the house, which was owned by her mother between Christmas and New Years in 1968. Ten small but active items they brought to their new house were a litter of hyperactive puppies. The puppies used to chase each other in a big circle beginning in the living room around a wall, through a hallway, into the dining room and back into the living room (brushing under a blanket hung between the rooms to keep down drafts).

One day, after several minutes of chasing each other around the lead puppy entered the dining room and abruptly "put on the breaks". The remaining puppies turned round the corner and ploughed into the lead one. As soon as they all stopped they huddled together and began yelping. After several seconds they all turned-tail and ran back into the living room. Jane and her mother ran into the dining room to see what had alarmed the dogs. They did not see or hear anything. The puppies did not venture back into the dining room for the rest of the day. Jane and her son moved out shortly after that.

In 1970 a newly married Jane and her husband moved in with her mother for a short while. She and her husband slept in a bedroom on the south end of the second floor. In the middle of the night her husband began screaming and thrashing around in bed and awakened her. She turned on the lights and saw that he was still asleep or only partially awake. She shook him for several seconds and he eventually sat up. She and asked him what was wrong. When he was able to talk he yelled; "it tried to kill me!"

After several moments he explained that in his dream the bedroom door opened and a cloaked and hooded figure entered. The figure approached the bed and stood over him and took out a long knife. He looked into the depths of the hood and saw burning red eyes, staring at him. The figure bent over him with the knife, which he grabbed. They fought for possession of it... at that point he began screaming and woke Jane. Although they slept in that room for several weeks, he never went to bed without the lights being left on.

Strangely enough Jane was not frightened. Her marriage was not a happy one and she feels that the ghost was acting like a guardian to her and was trying to frighten her husband away. Whether or not the ghost had anything to do with it, within a year Jane and her husband were divorced. She and her son found themselves living with her mother again. In 1972 Jane came home from a party around 1 AM. Her son and her mother were staying over at a friend's house. She had gone to the party with her brother, who had been staying in the house with them. She left the party before her brother and expected him to be

home very late. At 2 AM she heard the front door open and footsteps coming up the stairs. Thinking it was her brother she called out:
"Gerry, is that you?" There was no answer, but the footsteps continued past her brother's room toward hers in the south end of the house.

Her bedroom door opened and she repeated her question, "Gerry, is that you?"

Again there was no answer, but she saw a portion of a human head, silhouetted by the light in the hallway. She could not make out who it was; all she could see was part of a head, white skin and dark hair. The head withdrew without comment, the door closed and the footsteps went back down the hallway and stopped. Puzzled, but still unafraid, Jane went out into the hallway to see who had opened her door. The hallway was empty. She went down the stairs and checked the front door. It was closed and still locked (it was **always** kept locked). She had not heard it close when the footsteps stopped.

She searched the house looking first in her brother's room, then her mother's and every other room. There was no one in the house. Shrugging her shoulders Jane went back to bed. Shortly after that her brother came home. I asked her if how she could go back to sleep. She replied that the ghost had done nothing to hurt anyone. She thought it was just looking in on her to make sure she was all right. This was not the last experience her family had with their co-occupant.

In 1976 her ten year old son Karl was staying overnight with his grandmother. He remembers one incident that made his visit memorable. Sometime in the middle of the night he heard footsteps walking down the hallway on the second floor. Karl got up and went to the foot of the stairs when he heard the footsteps heading down toward him. When he reached the foot of the stairs he looked up. He could not see anyone in the dark, though he could hear the footsteps. He heard them walking all of the way down to the first floor and past him. They continued in the direction of front door. He watched the front door open and close without seeing anyone. That was too much for little Karl. He ran back into the living room and dove onto the couch and hid under the blankets. A few minutes later he heard the front door open, close and then heard footsteps walk across the hall and upstairs. Then silence.

The next morning he asked his grandmother if the house was haunted. In an offhand manner his grandmother told him; "Oh, it's just the ghost. Don't worry, he won't hurt you."

Karl has visited the house often in the last five or ten years. He went there a few years ago and found that it had been rented out to a group of college students as a kind of informal dorm house. He made it a point to ask the new tenants if they had ever had any experience with the ghost. At that point he was invited inside to talk to all of the residents. It turned out that all of the people living there at that time had had some kind of experience with the original tenant. This is especially true of the girl who had the bedroom on the south end of the second floor.

The White Eagle Tavern Revisited (836 N. Russell, Portland, OR)

One of the wonderful things about haunted houses (for authors) is that as time goes by the number of ghost stories continue to grow. This is especially true of Portland's most famous haunted drinking establishment. Shortly after I sent in the final draft *of Ghosts and Strange Critters of Washington and Oregon* to the printers, Chuck Hughes, the owner of the White Eagle told me that he was selling; (had already sold) the bar to McMenamins.

I was worried about McMenamins attitude towards ghosts and ghost book writers. I met with McMenamins full-time historian, Tim Hills, to discuss ghosts, ghost hunters, history and the *Corporate Line*. His attitude and that of McMenamins was positive about ghosts and my continuing to write about the White Eagle and other haunted properties owned by the Corporation. Tim has done extensive research on many of the properties that may shed more light on the hauntings at the White Eagle, which have continued, without dispelling them.

Shortly after the new staff began working at the White Eagle one of them was carrying supplies into the basement. He walked by the large freezer with his arms full of food. As he passed by the freezer, one of the doors came open and hit him in the back. This is a large restaurant freezer with doors that automatically latch when they are closed. It is possible that the last person who opened the freezer did not close the door completely which would not have latched properly. It is also possible but improbable, that the vibration of his passing had caused the door to swing open as he passed.

Another employee, Doug was serving drinks at the hundred-year-old bar. He felt a presence standing behind him. He did his best to ignore it. After ignoring the presence for several minutes began to feel a light touch on the back of it his head. It felt as if someone was teasing him by flicking the back of his head with a finger or blowing air on it. This happened several times. Finally Doug turned around and as he expected, there was no one there.

The White Eagle is so famous for it's ghostly legends that the manager; Bill has to field a lot of questions. In March of 1999 Bill was talking with a skeptical customer. The ghosts may have decided to make themselves known. A new fixture at the bar is a 12 inch mechanical bartender toy that dates to the 1950s that sits on the bar. It was designed to raise one arm holding a martini mixer, shake the arm and pour the martini into a glass held in the other arm and finally raise the glass. Although there were batteries in the toy it had not worked since it was brought to the bar. As soon as Bill finished talking about the ghost, the toy began to work.

The second floor of the White Eagle will be open soon to the general public as a bed and breakfast. Over the last 20 years there have been numerous leaks in the roof. A small crew of skilled carpenters has been busy removing the damaged fixtures, plaster and boards.

"When the work lights are on up there it's like daylight and I'm not frightened. But when the lights go off and I'm walking down the hallways it does get a little eerie, "the senior carpenter told me. Although he and his crew have not seen anything, they make it a point not to be upstairs at night.

The ghost who is supposed to haunt the upstairs of the White Eagle is that of Sam Worek. According to legend, Sam was supposed to have been left abandoned as a child in the neighborhood and the Hryszko (pronounced Risk-o') family took him in. Sam was supposed to have been a little slow or mildly retarded. When the Hryszko family closed the upstairs boarding rooms, Sam was one of the last tenants and died on the eve of his eviction. According to descendents of the original Hryszko family, Sam was an adult when he came to the White Eagle. He was an excellent cook with a weakness for the bottle. When he went on a "bender" he would disappear for days or weeks at a time. When he returned, he would go back to his kitchen, until the next time the bottle called. He was in his 60s or 70s when he died.

It may be that the ghost upstairs and elsewhere in the bar is not Sam, but another specter. People do not have to die in a building or place to haunt it. It may be that Sam has returned to clear his reputation or decided to stay in the place he called home for most of his life. There is a picture hanging in the bar taken around 1910. It shows the Hryszko family and an adult Sam posing for the camera. Sam is the dapper dark haired fellow with a lock of hair in his eyes staring at the camera. Some primitive people believe that pictures can steal or preserve a person's soul. Is some remnant of Sam's spirit looking at us?

Vancouver

The Vancouver Barracks

The Vancouver Barracks were founded in 1849 adjacent

to the Hudson's Bay Company's regional headquarters of Fort Vancouver. Many of the soldiers stationed there in the 1850s were northerners or Republicans. Young officers who became alumni of the Vancouver Barracks included George McClellan, U.S. Grant, Phillip Sheridan and many others. After the Civil War many other great and notable people who were stationed there or visited included Alfred Sully, O.O. Howard, Phillip Sheridan, Major Marcus Reno, George Marshall and many others.

Over the years there have been many changes in the size of the US Army post. Some of the original buildings have been destroyed and others have been constructed on their old sites. Major periods of construction date from the original construction of the early 1850s, then the 1880s, World War I and World War II and finally the mid-1970s. The last decade has seen the destruction or removal of several buildings.

In addition to these changes, the US Army presence has shrunk. Officer's Row, a series of residences built as housing for married officers and enlisted soldiers are no longer owned by the Army. The buildings are maintained as close to their original construction as possible and rented out as townhouses and small business offices. The Howard House, which was the old commander's residence, portions of the old parade ground and site of the Hudson's Bay Company National Monument are under the management of the National Park's Service.

Many of the old barracks buildings are currently used by Army Reserve units for their weekend drills. There are a few buildings still used by the active duty US Army component who still manage the facility. As long as they are there, the Vancouver Barracks is the oldest active duty Army post on the West Coast of the United States.

Building 638

Building 638 is currently being used as the Active Duty Army's headquarters building. It dates to the late 19th Century. Some of the strange happenings here include both sights and sounds. Soldiers who lived there temporarily were awakened to the sounds of reveille on the floor below. Footsteps and invisible bodies have walked past them, opening and closing doors. The sight of ghostly soldiers dressed in hundred year old uniforms playing billiards froze one soldier. One former post commander saw the apparition of a woman dressed in late 19th Century clothing walk into his office. When he searched his office he found it empty.

The following story happened in the summer of 1993. Cindy had been curious about the paranormal for several years. She was born in Clark County but moved away years before. Her mother sent her a series of newspaper articles on the ghosts in the Barracks and Cindy decided she to come home for vacation. She visited the old post hospital and arranged to spend the night there. After a few hours she was driven out of the building by unexplained thumping noises on the first floor and a powerful presence in the basement. Although she had been frightened in the old hospital, Cindy still wanted to spend the night in one of the buildings. The Post Commander had offered to let her stay in Building 638 and had given her a key.

She let herself into the building. Once she let herself into the building her flashlight died. It had worked earlier that evening. Cindy made her way through the dark to the Commander's office. She turned on the lights and left the door open so she could hear any strange noises. She unpacked her ghost-hunting equipment on a coffee table. This included a flashlight (non-functional), a voice activated tape recorder, a camera, notebook and pen and a Ouiji board. The clock read 11:15 PM as she settled down to her vigil. She read for a while and then decided to explore the building.

Her flashlight began working again and she used it to light her way down the building to the little museum that the Post maintained. She was halfway down the hallway when the flashlight went out again. She was able to find the lights switches to light up the museum room. After several minutes she turned off the lights and walked back to the Commander's

Office.

At 11:45, she had settled into the Commander's office again. She heard footsteps that sounded like someone was walking on the upper floor. Not above her, but in a different part of the building. This only lasted a few minutes. At 1:00 AM she heard the footsteps again. The building was quiet for nearly three hours. At 3:45 AM she heard a female voice singing a few notes to a song. Cindy could not tell what the voice sang. A few minutes later she heard the voice singing again. This time the song lasted a few seconds longer. Again, she could not tell what song the voice was singing.

She reached for her forgotten Ouiji board. She asked it if anyone was there. The board replied YES. She asked it for a name. The board spelled out the name EVE. This puzzled her because she had expected a male name, given the number of soldiers who had been stationed there.

Cindy continued her conversation with the board and spirit. She asked for a confirmation of the name. The board replied, YES-EVE. Cindy asked for a last name. All she got in reply were a few random consonants. She asked for the first name again. It replied, EVE. She said, "Eve what?" The board spelled out, GET-OUT-RUN-U-TRESPAS. She put the board away. This was not fun any more; she was becoming frightened again. She read her book for a little while and then settled down in a couch in the office and fell asleep.

She heard the sound of heavy boots on the walkway outside of the office, which was on the southeast corner of the building. They continued past the office window to the front entrance. They stopped outside the door and she heard the sound of a key turning in the lock. A few seconds later she heard the boots continue down the hallway toward the Commander's Office. Cindy stood up and looked at the door, waiting. It was only 4:00 AM. The Commander had told her that he would arrive in the morning much later than 0400 hours!

The sound of the boots halted on the other side of the door that had been blocked by the couch Cindy had been sleeping on. The doorknob twisted but of course the doors would not open. Cindy called out a "Good Morning!" She heard a man's voice reply that he could not get the door to open. She asked who he was.

"Private *****." She does not remember his name for sure. It could have been Nelson.

She heard him walk back outside the building and open the back door. He walked up to the Commander's Office. He paused in the entryway. Clutching her pepper spray, Cindy moved closer to get a better look. She saw a young man of around 18 years of age dressed in heavy black boots and dark green fatigue pants. He was below average height with his brown hair trimmed in a crew cut. She noticed that he had a pronounced gap between his teeth and acne on his cheeks and red blotches around his neck. She thought the red marks were "hickeys". His eyes were strange. They were so dark that the iris's appeared to be black.

He seemed to be very agitated. He asked who she was. She gave him her name and told him that she was there waiting for the ghost. She assumed that everyone knew about the ghost. He made no comment about that but asked if anyone else was there. He needed to check out some equipment because he was going to Korea.

Cindy moved closer to see if he smelled like alcohol. She thought he might have been drunk or on drugs. She did not smell alcohol. She was afraid. Four AM is a strange time to be checking out equipment. The Commander had not mentioned anything like this to her. Rather than telling him that she was alone, she told Nelson that there was a Sergeant around who would be back in a few minutes.

She went back to her book, in the hopes that he would leave. Instead he stood in the doorway, staring at her. She described it as the "creepiest" experience of her life. After several minutes of this he left without saying a word. He went out to the front porch and began pacing in front of the office where she was trying to read. After 15 minutes of pacing he came into the office again and asked where the bathroom was. Cindy told him there was one down the hall. She heard him walking down the hallway in his heavy boots. He came back in a few minutes and told her that all of the doors were locked. He asked her again about checking out some equipment.

The ritual began again. He stood in the hallway staring at her. Cindy tried a different approach. She tried to be nice and calm him down. She started asking him questions about himself. He told her that he was from Virginia and he was looking forward to some event that was happening in the next week. He was fortunate because in two weeks he was shipping out to Korea. They talked for a few more minutes and then he said he had to go. Before he left he repeated one more time that he had to check out some equipment.

Cindy fell asleep shortly after he left. She talked with the Commander about her night when he arrived later that morning. When she described the strange soldier the Commander became more attentive and began shaking his head. He asked for a more detailed description of the private. He told her that no one should have been at the building that early and more importantly, no one should have had a key to the building. He was concerned enough to do his own investigation.

A few weeks later Cindy received a note from the Commander. He had three major pieces of information. Firstly, no soldiers assigned to the Vancouver Barracks were being reassigned to Korea. Secondly, the locks on the building had been replaced six months before and the front and back doors needed separate keys to open them. Only a few designated people had one key, much less keys to both doors. Finally he told her that several years ago, his office had been used as a supply room. It had been converted to an office in the early 1980s.

Was this the ghost of a long departed soldier? Cindy's information supports a belief that this was not a soldier assigned to the Vancouver Barracks. The man was wearing heavy boots and dark green fatigue pants. This was the wrong uniform for the 1990s. The US Army phased in the current camouflage pattern fatigues in the early 1980s. Prior to that the Army uniform from around 1977 to the early 1980s was a light green permanent press uniform we used to call Pickle Suits. From the 1950s through the 1970s the fatigue uniform was a heavy, dark green cotton uniform called Sateen's. Based on Cindy's description, this soldier was dressed anywhere from 15 - 30 years out of date.

The Vancouver Barracks Headquarters Building

The Clark County Historical Museum (15th and Main Street, Vancouver, WA)

The museum was constructed in 1909, as the Vancouver City Library. It was built with donations from the Carnegie Foundation, the Hidden family and other local contributors. The only complaint made was that it was located too far from downtown Vancouver to be convenient for many patrons. With the construction of the Fort Vancouver Regional Library in the early 1960s, the Carnegie Library was converted into a museum. The museum is open Tuesdays through Saturdays, from 1:00 - 5:00 PM. It has artifacts from historical figures like Andrew Jackson and U. S. Grant to everyday tools used by ordinary people.

Some volunteers have reported strange happenings at night. On the 28th of March 1996 my wife Janine and I stayed overnight in the basement of the museum. There are three separate rooms down there; the Railroad room; an open visitor's room and an artifact storage room. We spent some time looking in the basement. We did not notice anything strange or feel any unearthly presences.

We had a few moments of stress when we heard the sound of heavy breathing in the railroad room. This turned out to be part of the audio exhibit of a railroad telegraph station. In this display, there is the sound of the telegraph key and the breathing of the operator can also be heard.

We brought a cassette tape recorder with us, and recorded part of the evening. When I listened to the tape, I heard myself get up to investigate the sound and return to my wife. Strangely enough, while we were talking, there was a low but distinct sound on the tape that neither one of us heard while we were there. Low, but clear; *the sound of quick, and pant-like breathing*. Breathing that did not resemble the sound of the railroad display.

The Hidden House (100 West 13th, Vancouver, Washington)

Anyone walking through downtown Vancouver will note the large number of buildings built of red brick. Most of this brick came from the Hidden Brick Co.'s furnaces. Lowell M. Hidden was an early influence in Clark County. He opened his brick company and began producing bricks in 1871. Through a combination of planning, hard work and luck his business thrived. Lowell Hidden built the Hidden house in 1884. It is a fine brick Victorian style house with some unique decorative touches added by the Danish craftsmen who finished its interior. In addition to being the Hidden family residence, it served as the first home of Clark Community College and now is open to the public as a restaurant. It is also haunted.

The ghost or ghosts seem to be active at all times of the day. One morning, an employee was mopping up in the front entry when she heard a woman singing. The only problem with the singing was that the employee was alone in the building. One evening, another employee who was a skeptic had a spectral incident.

He was in the upstairs dining room vacuuming the floor when he heard his name called. He was alone in the building as well. He stopped and listened. The only other people with keys were the owner and the manager. It was neither of their voices. He resumed cleaning and heard his name called again. He stopped and called out. There was no answer. He started vacuuming again; and heard the voice a third time. He left and never entered the building alone again.

One day the ghost decided to monopolize the employee restroom. During an employee meeting, the bathroom door was found locked. The manager took a head count. All of the employees were present. After knocking, and receiving no answer, the door was forced open. The restroom was empty and locked from the inside. Aside from this incident, this ghost has never been seen nor done any harm. So if you want to use the restroom and it is locked, be courteous; it may be *occupied!*

Works Consulted

Books

Alley, B.F. and J.P. Munro-Fraser

1983 *Clarke County Washington Territory 1885.* Post Publishing Co., Camas WA.

Clark County Genealogical Society,

1989 *Clark County Pioneers.* Clark County Genealogical Society, Vancouver, WA.

Corning, Howard McKinley (editor)

1952 *Oregon, End of the Trail.* Binfords & Mort, Portland, OR.

Jollata, Pat

1993 *Naming Clark County.* Fort Vancouver Historical Societyof Clark County, Vancouver, WA.

Van Arsdol, Ted

1991 *Northwest Bastion the U.S. Army Barracks at Vancouver, 1849-1916.* The Heritage Trust of Clark County, Vancouver, WA.

Vokac, David

1987 *The Great Towns of the Pacific Northwest.* West Press, Seattle, WA.

Periodicals

Anonymous

1 November 1988 "Ghosts may lurk in history's rooms". *The Columbian*, Vancouver, WA.

Anonymous,
1992 40th Anniversary Memorial Service Honoring Sgt. First Class Jerome F. Sears.
Anonymous
Cullier, David
24 June 1997b "Ghost Stories Flitting Around Barracks". *The Columbian*, Vancouver, WA
No Date "Ghost Stories Haunt Vancouver". The *Columbian*, Vancouver, WA.
Gosrsky, Eric
17 October 1995 "Palace of faded elegance", The *Oregonian*, Portland, OR.
Mahar, Ted
31 October 1988 "Ghost Stories". *Oregonian*, Portland, OR.
Mandel, Michelle
27 May 1998 "Keeper of the ghost". *Oregonian*, Portland, OR, pp. E2.
Maves, Norm Jr.
12 January 1995 "Story behind a sign: Portland soldier's Korean War sacrifice", the *Oregonian*, Portland, Oregon.
Mendoza, Lori
31 October 1996 "Shadows of the Past". *Oregonian*, Portland, OR.
Oppegaard, Brett and Pat Jollata
27 October 1995, "Reflections a look back at Clark County's History", the *Columbian*, Vancouver Washington.
Pollard, Royce E.
"Typical Pioneers and Builders of Clarke County". *Clark County History*, Vol. 22, pp. 53-77. Fort Vancouver Historical Society, of Clark County, Inc., Vancouver, WA.
Rubenstein, Sura
31 October 1995 "While Little Ghosts and Goblins Wander in Search of Candy, Real Sprits May be Afoot in Portland". *Oregonian*, Portland, OR.

Internet sources

Brenna
1997 "Whistling boy", in the *International Ghost Hunter Society* web site www.ghosts.org/stories.html.
Haas, Barbara
1998 The Old Storm House (Strum), in the *International Ghost Hunter Society* web site, www.ghosts.org/stories.html.
Smith, Jamie,
1998 "Scratching Sounds", *ww.ghosts.org.stories.html.*

Western Oregon

Salem, Oregon

The Thompson Road House, (the corner of Liberty and Madrona, Salem, Oregon)

In 1905 Fred Thompson built a house in Salem for his parents Frederick and Maria Thompson. Frederick Franklin was an old man at that time and had served in the Civil war yeaars before. After Frederick and Maria died the house was sold to a succession of owners until 1965. In 1965, Jack Beck purchased the house and renovated the interior, turning it into a decorating business. The house used as a business for 10 years until it was turned into a residence again. It was sold to McMenamins in the late 1980s, who turned it into a small brewery and public house. It opened for business in 1990.

Sue was one of the employees at the Franklin house when it first opened for business. She worked there from 1990 to 1992. She noticed the house was "creaky" the first day. A few weeks later, Sue and her co-worker Becky were doing the books after closing. They were sitting in the hallway chatting as they did the accounts. They heard the sound of the cash register turning on. They went into the bar and found that it was indeed turned on. This type of cash register needs to have the key inserted and turned to complete a circuit and turn on. The key was in the lock, but in the "off" position. After several key turnings and button pushings, they managed to turn the cash register off. They finished their work and prepared to leave. As they walked to the door, they heard a click and saw that the restaurant coffee machine had just switched itself on. They did not stop to turn it off before they left.

It did not take long for the rest of the employees to figure out that that they had a playful ghost. They called him Franklin after the houses first occupant. Many people, employees and customers have felt cold breezes brush past them as they walked up the stairs. One customer came into the building for the first time, walked up the front steps, stopped and turned to face Sue. With a smile she asked Sue if the house was haunted.

The second floor seems to be a focus for paranormal activity. Many people have heard a tapping noise coming from the cupboard door of an old linen closet on the second floor. Becky was taking an order from customers sitting in the booth over the front porch. A man with silver gray hair, wearing brown slacks and a brown sweater almost brushed into her when he walked through the doorway into the room next to her. She glanced up and told him that she would be with him in a minute. She finished taking the order and turned sideways to face the other room. It was empty. There was not way he could have left without brushing by her again. Many people have felt strange in this room. Maybe it has something to do with the portrait of Mad King Ludwig on the wall.

Sue found that Franklin was not confined to the second floor. She went to the brewers building on an errand, when she saw a man with gray-brown hair, wearing a brown sweater and pants. He was half concealed behind a shed door. When she walked over to find out what he was doing, she found that the shed was empty. She saw him several times. He would frequently hide in the shadows and show himself to get her attention and then hide again.

Each time she thought she had him cornered, he would disappear. He would frequently smile at her and wave before going into hiding. One day when she saw the strange man run behind a building she had someone with her. She placed this person on one side of the building while she walked around the other. Both stepped around the corner at the same time, only to confront each other. The man had vanished. Later she watched him through a window as he entered a building. As she watched him walk around the building, she saw him disappear, with a bright but not blinding flash of light.

Despite the difference in hair color, Sue and Becky

believe that they saw the same man. Perhaps when he is outside Franklin prefers to look a little younger. That way he can move a little bit easier when he hides from people. The Thompson family still lives in Salem. Occasionally they come to visit the old family home. Sue was talking with one female descendent, describing all of the strange things that had been happening.

"Oh", the woman exclaimed. "That sounds just like Grandfather.!

The white cat and the dark man (Private residence near the corner of 18th and Nebraska, Salem, Oregon)

I was sitting in the Thompson Road House talking to some of the staff about strange goings-on there when one of the patrons offered me his story. Ron and his family moved into an old house on Nebraska Street, near it's intersection with East 18th. The house was built several decades ago, when the area was used as farmland. He was five years old at the time and lived there for nearly 20 years. During those years he saw some very strange things.

The first incident happened shortly after moving into the house. Their black cat, Midnight had a litter of black kittens. All of the cats were black except for one white kitten. One morning the white kitten was injured and had to be put down. Ron watched his father bury the dead kitten in the back yard. That night Ron was playing in the doorway of his room when he heard a cat meow. He turned his head and looked out of his doorway at the stairs. He saw a white kitten peeking at him over the top of the stairwell. It jumped up to the top of the stairs and walked into the bathroom. Ron got up and followed it into the bathroom. It was empty.

Ron became very interested in alternative religions and magic as well as ghosts. When he was 15, Ron and his friends were watching television in the living room. Before his mother left for work that morning she had told him that she wanted the dishes done before she came home. Like most teenagers, Ron ignored her and continued to watch television with his friends.

When his mother returned he rushed out into the kitchen to belatedly finish his chores, only to find that the dishes had been done.

Ron's interest in the strange became darker, until one night. When he was a junior in high school, he was studying in his bedroom. He had moved down to the first floor. After some time he felt as if he was being watched. He turned around and looked at the basement door. It was partially opened. He saw a man standing on the basement stairs, partially hidden by the door, which opened inward. The figure was all black but was three dimensional, like a man wearing an all-over leotard.

Ron froze. He stared at the man for several seconds in fear. When he was able to move he. got up and ran at the door, kicking it completely open (and hopefully pinning the man hiding behind it). He turned and ran across his room and jumped out the window and ran to a friend's house. He stayed there several hours before he returned home and searched his room and the basement. Ron believed that his dark thoughts had acted as a magnet to attract other dark forces to him.

That incident marked a change in Ron's attitude and life. He gave up all interest in the occult and took to wearing a crucifix around his neck. A few weeks later he was glad for the symbol he was wearing. He was in his room again when he heard the sound of a woman screaming. At first he thought the noise was coming from outside. It became progressively louder. He realized that the noise was coming from the house, from inside his room. He reached for his cross but found that his arm was paralyzed. After several seconds of internal struggle he was able to move his arm. He grabbed the cross hanging around his neck. The noise stopped.

It left Ron a changed person. It also caused him to speculate on the nature of human beings and how they react to the paranormal. This series of incidents changed his life for the better. He wonders how many people would experience the same thing and perhaps reform for a few hours or days, but will eventually fall back on their old ways and ignore the warnings?

Springfield, Oregon

The Haunted Trunk (Private residence in Springfield, Oregon)

In the early 1960s a Mrs. Weaver and her son moved into a rental house in Springfield. The house was several decades old and included remnants of possessions of several past tenants. Like the old trunk she found in the attic when she moved in. The Weavers were moving some of their possessions into the attic when they saw the trunk. They opened the trunk out of curiosity but did not find anything interesting inside. After closing the trunk they moved it aside and put some of their own boxes in its place. That night they heard the sound of footsteps in the attic. When they investigated the noise they did not see anyone but did notice the lid of the trunk was now opened.

Nearly every night they heard the sound of footsteps walking in the empty attic. When they investigated they never found anyone. They would find that the trunk, which had been closed was now open; or if it was opened before, it was now closed. Sometimes the noise was so loud that the Weavers turned on the radio to cover the noise of the ghostly footsteps. They had several visitors who also heard the sounds of ghostly pacing. Strangely enough, they tried to record the sound of disembodied footsteps several times. Each time the tape recorder picked up all of the normal sounds in the house, except the footsteps.

The sounds became so frightening that the Weavers moved out for a short time. They returned and decided to try and figure out a solution. They experimented first by closing the trunk and moving it back to the same place where they found it. That did the trick. The noises stopped and the trunk remained closed. Weaver admitted she was tempted to move the trunk again to see if the noises would start again…but decided not to.

Sources Consulted

Periodicals

Keefer, Bob

14 July 1991 "Another Roadside Attraction", the *Register Guard*, Eugene, Oregon.

Obrien, Mike

27 October 1975 "Is anybody up there?" *Register Guard*, Eugene, OR, pp. E1.

Unknown

5 May 1968 "Springfield haunted house quiets down", *Register Guard*, Eugene, Oregon.

Western Washington and the Puget Sound

The Pacific Northwest is full of towns founded by people with high hopes in the middle of the 19th century. They were all trying to attract the same businesses to their settlements; shipping, lumber mills, farming and most importantly railroads. Without the railroads it did not matter how much lumber was cut, how many fish were caught or how much food was grown. It could not be moved to outside markets without the railroads. Towns that were able to attract railroads grew into major cities like Seattle and Tacoma. Towns that were not able to build a railroad depot in those early days eventually died or faded into obscurity.

Bellevue, WA

The White Lady (Private residence in Bellevue, WA)

In 1990 Jeff's family moved to Bellevue. They liked their new home and moved in without any strange incidents. It was not until 1994 that Jeff began to notice anything strange. He began to see a white figure, walking across the hallways. It moved so quick that at first he thought he was seeing things. He began to realize otherwise when it began to appear regularly. He told his parents about it but they did not comment on it at first. Later they admitted that they had seen it to.

Despite the original shock none of them felt threatened by the white apparition. They felt that it was a good spirit and began referring to it as the White Lady. The Lady may have appeared for some purpose. In 1995 Jeff began seeing a shadowy black figure walking through the house. Where the White Lady moved quickly, this figure appeared to walk quite slowly.

One night Jeff was having trouble sleeping. He looked up from his bed and saw the black figure slowly walking toward him. Jeff became quite frightened as the figure came closer.

Before he could yell for his parents the White Lady quickly appeared. It seemed to stop the black figure and lead it away. Jeff never saw the black spirit after that, although the White Lady continued to appear.

Centralia, WA

The Olympic Club (112 N Tower Avenue, Centralia, Washington)

Shortly after the turn of the century, Jack Scuitto (pronounced Suto) left his bar in Victoria B.C. and moved to western Washington. The reason for this move is unknown, but it must have been an important one. He left a successful business in rich, urban Canada to relocate in rough and ready Lewis County. At first he tried to open a bar in Centralia but his request was turned down because the city fathers felt there were too many bars in Centralia.

In June of 1908 a fire ravaged portions of downtown Centralia, destroying several businesses. Scuitto purchased a burned out a lot and built the Olympic Club. Because of the rush to rebuild, it was not fancy, but the customers did not seem to mind. The Olympic's clientele consisted mostly of lumberjacks and mill workers for several years until if was remodeled in 1913. A major fixture was the large mahogany bar was installed. In addition to the bar, several Tiffany style lampshades and wall mosaics were added. Strangely enough, the new theme for this working man's club was tulips.

In 1916, the United States began the great experiment known as Prohibition. This meant the death of many of Centralia's bars and clubs. Scuitto survived by expanding into the vacant business space next to his bar. He added café and billiard tables, which are still there. The café counter still has the high-backed oak chairs that spin round. There is evidence that the hotel next to his bar was also a place of "negotiable" affection. Patrons at the bar could contact the hotel manager by intercom to see if there was a friendly lady free in the hotel. The Olympic Club was a men's only club until 1972. Although women and children were welcome in the café, they were not welcome in the bar. This contributed to rumors of strange or illegal doings within the bar by those who were not allowed inside.

Like many small towns in the United States, Centralia and the Olympic Club have their own mysteries. Did the International Workers of the World (known as the IWW or Wobblies) plan the *Centralia Massacre* on Armistice Day in 1919 over drinks in Olympic Club? Did Joseph Scuitto, as a member of the local business community report them? Or was he sympathetic to their cause? We will never have the answer to those questions, since the historic record of the events of Armistice Day, 1919 are not talked about in Centralia.

In 1996 McMenamins purchased the Olympic Club. They cleaned and repaired some of the internal fixtures and wiring without removing any of the Olympic's charm. They even left the huge, monolithic urinals in the men's restroom. When the Olympic was re-opened in 1997, the ceremonies included bagpipers playing for good luck. The manager, Chad Cooper reported that a former employee saw the ghost of a man standing by the large cast iron stove, watching the ceremony. The ghost, nick-named Elmer has been seen standing there several times. Some patrons have reported that their chairs have moved without human aid. The burglar alarm has also gone off when no one has been in the bar.

I visited the Olympic Club in the spring of 1999 and spoke with several employees. The ghost still seems to be there, though he may have changed his activities. Several employees have said that they sometimes hear a man's laughter echo throughout the building when they are there alone in the evenings. Lisa, a server at the bar has felt a presence following her around the bar, even into the restroom. The bartender Aaron, clearly recalls a recent event.

A few months before my visit, two customers were sitting at the bar, near the entrance. They called Aaron over and asked if the bar was haunted. These were not regular customers, so he was surprised that they would ask. He replied that the Olympic had that kind of reputation…The men explained that a few minutes earlier they heard the nearby double doors open. They felt the breeze of someone walking into the bar behind them. The problem was, they were facing the large mirror behind the bar and did not see the reflection of anyone walking behind them. Aaron and other workers have noticed possible paranormal activity in the second floor balcony at the back of the bar.

On two separate occasions, Aaron has turned off the lights in the balcony after cleaning up there and then returned to the bar. After reaching the bar he has looked up and saw that the balcony lights had been turned on again. Kelly, another employee seen the same thing as well. In a separate incident, Kelly was in the bar, standing next to the wood stove. He saw a man wearing a white shirt walking in the back of the bar. The man disappeared into the stairway leading to the balcony. Kelly waited for the man to exit onto the balcony. After five minutes Kelly went to the back of the bar and climbed the stairs onto the balcony. The stairs and balcony were empty.

McMenamins historian Tim Hills remains skeptical about the paranormal but is interested enough to suggest a possible identity for Elmer. He believes that in life, Elmer may have been Louis Galba. Galba was a German butcher who came to Centralia around the turn of the Century. He rented a room at a hotel that used to stand on the site of the Olympic Club. When the hotel caught fire in 1908, Galba was trapped in his second floor room. After being severely burned, Galba jumped to the ground below, where he broke several bones and suffered severe internal injuries. Galba was hospitalized for three months before he finally died. Construction began on the Olympic Club shortly after that. Does Louis Galba return to his ghostly room every night after a hard day's work?

Everett, WA

The Spirit of Discord? (A private residence in Everett, WA)

There is a fairly common theme found in some haunted houses. Some houses seem to remember past events, including pain, sorrow and anger and store it up over time. When ordinary, happy people move into these affected, or afflicted houses their moods and behavior begin to change. In some cases they repeat past events and act out the tragedies that occurred decades before. Oftentimes there does not seem to be an active intelligence, just a feeling of oppression or rage. This story from Everett seems to be an example of this kind of haunting.

In 1992 Robin moved into a large rental house with her two friends, Josh and Chuck. Robin and Chuck were best friends and had known each other for several years. The two of them had known Josh for several years and all got along. They were in their early 20's and were all set to enjoy their first big adult experience, a place of their own! The wonder and positive thrill did not last long.

Almost immediately after moving in they all began

experiencing personality changes. Trivial disagreements could lead to shouting matches. None of them seemed able to get to sleep without a drink first. When they did sleep, they would be awakened by nightmares. Robin and Chuck used to talk over all of their problems, now they began to avoid each other. Parties seemed to end in violent disagreements. The house seemed to be filled with malice. Robin began to keep to her room.

After living there for two months Robin was in her room, which was over the front porch, reading a book. She put it down when she heard someone run up the front porch and open the door. She listened as the door slammed and heavy footsteps walked across the entry way. She heard a low voice or voices whispering. It was early afternoon. Robin thought it was Chuck home from work early.

As she left her room and walked to the head of the stairs to greet him she called out his name. There was no answer. She lost her smile of welcome as all of the hair on her arms stood up on end. There was no answer, no sound. She walked down the stairs to the first stairway landing. She called to Chuck again. Again, there was no answer. She looked around the corner to the entry hallway. It was empty. At first she froze with terror then turned and ran back up to her room. When Chuck finally came home she was so relieved that she nearly cried.

After that she began to hear voices from the front of the house and the dining room. The voices were usually too low to make out what was being said. On one occasion she heard someone or something calling her name from the first floor. After that incident, whenever Robin came home she would announce her presence as soon as she came through the front door. She would also ask whatever powers were in the house to cease their activity. She kept her bedroom window open all the time. That way she could hear the outside world instead of focusing on the things inside the house. She tried to exorcise or keep the spirits of the house out of her and Chuck's rooms by burning sage and saying prayers in their rooms. Despite her activities Robin did not discuss her experiences with Chuck or

Josh. Things only continued to get worse.

Finally after six months of living in their dream house, Robin, Chuck and Josh moved out. Robin and Chuck found another house and continued as room mates for another four years until Chuck became engaged and moved out to find another house with his fiancée. Despite the good times that they shared, Chuck and Robin never talk about their first house and prefer it that way.

Treasure Island and the King on the Equator (10th Street Boat Dock, Everett, WA)

The *Equator* is an 81 foot, two masted schooner that used to be moored in Everett Harbor. I try to visit the site of each haunting if it is possible, to ensure the building is still there and perhaps gather more information. In this case, I did not have the time to visit Everett to see if the ship was still there or if there is any new information about the ship. Joan Bingham and Dolores Riccio have written a long article about strange happenings aboard her (see the ***sources consulted*** at the end of this section).

The *Equator* was constructed in the late 1880s for trading along the South Pacific. There is a great amount of lore surrounding the ship. There are stories of strange people being sighted on her deck and workmen's tools disappearing. As well as floating lights seen above her decks. This led to her caretakers allowing a séance to be held on the Equator.

During the Séance two glowing lights appeared over the stern of the ship. These lights floated down to hover near the psychics. After the séance the psychics gave details of their experiences. They stated that the two glowing lights were the ghosts of Robert Louis Stevenson and King Kalakaua of Hawaii. The former was the author of books like *Kidnapped* and *Treasure Island*. The latter man was the last king of Hawaii and father of Queen Liliuokalani, Hawaii's last queen. It is hard to believe that a world famous author and a Hawaiian King had anything to do with a freighter, but it there was indeed a historic association between these two men and the Equator.

Stevenson came to the South Seas in the 1880s. His suffered from tuberculosis and other health problems, brought on by the Industrial Revolution in Great Britain. He found that his health improved in while travelling in less industrialized settings. He spent several months living in a large house at Waikiki. While he was living there he was a frequent guest in the palace of Hawaii's king, Kalakaua.

King Kalakaua's reign straddled the period between independent native rule and the nationalistic pressure of American landowners. He tried to European-ize his country and included some democratic reforms, as well as increase the power and prestige of the throne. His hospitality was famous and Stevenson was a frequent guest at the royal dinner table.

After several months the heat and humidity of Hawaii affected Stevenson's health. He booked passage on the *Equator* for himself and his family. King Kalakaua, his cabinet, family and the royal band escorted the Stevenson party on their way and had a final luncheon on the ship. The Stevenson's lived aboard the ship for six months, sailing along as supercargo, visiting the regular ports of call. Eventually they made port in Samoa where Stevenson purchased a large estate and settled there. He died there on December 3rd, 1894. His mother saw Stevenson's ghost on her deathbed in 1897. His ghost has been reported on his estate as late as the 1970s.

Stevenson being a romantic Scot, almost certainly believed in ghosts. Ghosts are a part of Pacific Island life as well. King Kalakaua would have also believed in his ability to survive as a spirit. It is not surprising that the two of them might take the opportunity to meet again in this place where they both shared goodwill and fellowship.

Fort Lewis, Washington

Fort Lewis, Washington is one of the largest US Army posts in the United States. Along with the main post, Fort

Lewis controls facilities in Yakima, Hunter Ligget, Camp Parks (both in California) and the Vancouver Barracks. Together these posts take up 86,721 acres of woodlands, prairies and lakes with 691 miles of roads. Fort Lewis is a small city, with restaurants, stores, banks, taxi and bus service, schools, libraries, hospital and recreation facilities, serving nearly 19,000 soldiers and 5,000 civilian employees.

In 1917 the citizens of Pierce County enacted a $2 million bond and bought 70,000 acres of land. They donated the land to the federal government to establish a military reservation. The new facility was named Camp Lewis in honor of Meriwether Lewis. Construction began in May of 1917. In three months workmen finished construction of 2,179 buildings and structures all with electricity. The Main Gate was built of field stone and squared logs to resemble the old military block houses.

As Fort Lewis grew larger it swallowed up several old pioneer land claims. The houses were gone but the cemeteries remained. In most cases the Army tried to preserve the cemeteries. Soldiers involved in training exercises often encounter several small cemeteries with a half dozen graves surrounded by wrought iron fences in the middle of nowhere. Unfortunately, the Army was not able to identify and protect all of the cemeteries. Some may have been covered over by later construction, like the Centurion Playhouse near the main entrance to Fort Lewis.

In the early 1970s Rick was a high school freshman. He became a member of an amateur theater group that put on several plays a year at the old theater. He did this mostly as a way of pursuing romantic interests with some female members of the theater group. One evening he was working late hanging stage lights. He was standing on the top of a ladder, about 25 feet above the stage. To assist in aiming the stage lights, all of the house lights were off. Rick had been at this for some time when he felt a tap on his shoulder and heard a voice say, "hello".

This startled him, since he was standing at the top of the

ladder. He turned around and saw a male figure from the waist up. The figure was eye to eye with him. It was a man, dressed in a flannel shirt and suspenders with a full beard and uncombed hair. Rick was frightened but he somehow made it down the ladder without falling and ran out of the theater. He jumped into his car and drove away. When he left the main gate and headed north on Interstate 5, Rick drove past the theater, on the other side of the fence separating Fort Lewis from the freeway. All of the lights were on in the building and the doors were open.

Rick stopped by his boss's house and told him the story. They drove to the theater together to close it properly. They found the theater in the condition that Rick had described to him. At that point Rick's boss told him that he and other people had experienced incidents similar to the one Rick had just suffered.

After that incident Rick took more notice of strange things around him. During one performance he was in the front of the theater, near the audience seating. He watched the doors leading to the balcony seating start to swing back and forth with no one standing near them. He watched this for a few minutes and checked other doors in that part of the theater. They were swinging on their own as well. After the play was over, people backstage noticed that doors in their area were swinging back and forth.

Rick liked to walk across the empty stage when the theater was empty. Sometimes he would feel someone on the other side of the stage curtains when he brushed against them. He would tell himself that a draft was blowing the curtains against him. On other occasions he would hear voices or rustling noises on the stage. When he investigated, the stage was empty.

According to the Theater Company, the theater had been built in World War II, on top of an old pioneer cemetery. This accounted for the appearance of the ghost that Rick saw. Visitors to Fort Lewis today will not be able to visit the Centurion Theater. It was torn down at the end of the Vietnam

War. I contacted the Ft. Lewis historian's office regarding the Centurion Theater. Unfortunately there are no records or maps showing its exact location. A series of on-post housing for soldiers with families has been constructed on that portion of Fort Lewis. The Army is too practical not to re-use a site with utilities already installed. I wonder if the current workers or residents have similar problems.

Morton, Washington

The St. Helen's Manor House (7476 Hwy 12, Morton, WA)

When Susyn Dragness purchased the St. Helen's Manor House Bed and Breakfast approximately five years ago she had no idea that she might have had one or two permanent guests. Unlike many haunted houses where the ghosts fade over time, her ghosts seem to be as active as ever. Her home has been featured in several newspaper articles, as well as a 1996 Halloween news feature on King County's Channel 5 television.

My wife and I stayed in her comfortable 1910s home in April of 1999. We appreciated being treated more like long lost cousins rather than customers. Susyn showed us a copy of the video from the news visit. When they visited, Channel 5 brought a psychic from Ireland who had no prior knowledge of the house. The psychic said that she detected the presence of two women, a mother and daughter. She also felt there had been a murder in the house. The psychic said several prayers for the spirits of the dead in the hopes of exorcising them. Several days after the visit Susyn was surprised to find the psychic returning to the house for a follow up visit. Neither visit seems to have worked.

One of the regular aspects of this haunting is the way the fire door on the stairs closes all on its own. When the house was converted into a B&B, fire codes required a fire door be installed. This door is spring loaded so that it will normally close. It is held open by an Electro-magnet attached to the wall.

If the electricity goes out, the magnetic field cuts out and the door slams shut. At the St. Helen's Manor house the door shuts on it's own nearly every night at precisely 4:20 AM. When Channel 5 visited Susyn, they placed a remote camera in the stairwell. The tape shows the door slamming shut at...4:20 AM. The television station brought an electrician who examined the locking mechanism. He could find nothing wrong with the lock. There was nothing wrong with the other three locks that Susyn had replaced earlier.

When Susyn first moved in, she came home one day to find the house filled with the scent of lilac perfume. Around the same time, she moved the piano in the living room away from the wall to clean behind it. When she began scrubbing the walls she was frightened when she was hit on the head by several drops of water. They seemed to come from thin air. She looked up, but there were no leaking pipes and the ceiling was dry and unstained. She stopped trying to clean behind the piano and the indoor rain ceased.

The guest bedrooms are all located on the second floor. There is the pink room, the blue room, and the green room. They all seem to have their own ghostly character. One night a couple stayed in the green room. The husband woke his wife up in the middle of the night. He complained to his wife that the heavy scent of lilac perfume was nearly suffocating him.

In 1995 Susyn had two female guests who had requested separate beds. Unfortunately, they were forced to share the full sized bed in the pink room. Around 9:30 PM Susyn heard a loud crashing and banging coming from their room. She thought that the two women, (who were very large) had broken the bed. She knocked on the door and asked if they were all right. They replied (in irritated tones) that they were just painting their toenails. Susyn left, embarrassed.

Early the next morning one of the women was in the hallway bathroom when she heard a loud crashing noise coming from the pink room. She bumped into Susyn, who was in the hallway as she ran out of the bathroom. The two of them burst into the pink room, afraid that the other woman had fallen down. They found her standing by the bed, calmly packing her bags. Everything was in its place.

The blue room is the most famous haunted room. Everyone who knows about the hauntings wants to sleep there. Many people wake up in the night sensing a presence, though no one has seen it. A couple was staying there when a hand shook the husband hard enough to wake him up in the middle of the night. In 1997 or 1998 a Native American woman travelling south stopped at the Manor House. While she was there, Susyn heard the sounds of glass breaking and rumblings as if furniture was being thrown around. Her past experience in the pink room stopped Susyn from bursting in to see what was happening.

The next morning Susyn escorted the woman to her car and then ran into the house to check the room. Although the bed was rumpled, everything was in its place and nothing was broken. She did notice one strange thing. The garbage can was full of clothing wrappers and labels. Apparently the woman had bought all new clothing the day before and unpacked it in her room. Susyn had noticed that her guest's car had been brand new as well. It's white leather interior had been painted with various Native American pictographic symbols. Susan was convinced that the woman had been running from something and starting a new life. Unfortunately whatever she was running from had energized the spirits in the blue room and probably followed her to her next stop.

The night I stayed there, my wife and I slept in the blue room. Nothing out of the ordinary happened in our room. This is not unusual; most ghosts do not perform on command. At 4:20 AM I was awakened when the fire door did slammed shut. The next morning over breakfast Susyn told me the story of her house.

John Uden constructed the house over a two year period, from 1908 - 1910. He built it for his mail order bride Anna. It took two years, because she refused to leave Austria until everything was perfect. Finally Anna Senn and her daughter

Anna arrived. John lived quite happily with his new family for several years until his death a decade or so later. Young Anna became a local schoolteacher until she married Clarence Fisher. After their marriage young Anna was forced to stop teaching school and they moved in with her widowed mother. Within a year or two the elder Anna died suddenly after drinking a glass of herbal tea with her daughter. This left the couple alone in the house. For a few years.

A few years after Anna Senn died, Clarence Fisher's father died and his mother moved in with Clarence and Anna. She lived with them for a few months until she too died, after drinking herbal tea with Anna. Clarence died a few years after that. Rumor has it that Clarence, (who used to drink Sherry with the family dog on the front porch) died of cirrhosis of the liver. At that point Anna became the schoolteacher for Morton again. She remained a solid citizen and was beloved by the community until her death many years later.

When Susyn was telling this story, the house was quiet as my wife and I listened with our full attention. When she reached the point where she described Anna's mother-in-law death, the fire door slammed shut. From personal experience I can tell you, the reader that there is such a thing as coincidence. But sometimes coincidence is just too big of a word to fit situations like this.

Olympia, Washington

The little boy blue (The Governor's mansion, 501 13th Avenue SW, Olympia, Washington)

In the 1960s Albert Rosellini was governor of Washington State. My father remembers this very well because he and many other state employees were worried that they would be fired in a massive downsizing. Fortunately for my childhood prosperity, that did not happen.

During Rosellini's administration Leon Thompson and

several other people went on a tour of the Governor's mansion. While they were taking the tour his group saw a boy wearing a sailor suit riding an antique tricycle. Some of the tourists even waved at the little boy. Later they asked their tour guide who the little boy was. The guide froze at their question and at first refused to answer. Later they heard the sound of a bouncing ball. The tour guide finally told them that the ghosts of two little boys haunt the mansion. In the 1970s there was construction at the mansion and the little boy on the tricycle disappeared.

According to Thompson, the sound of the bouncing ball is still heard. Mary Charles, the mansions executive coordinator, disputed this in 1997. She stated that she had never experienced anything extraordinary nor had the chef or the housekeeper, both long-term mansion employees.

Tours of the Governor's mansion are conducted on Wednesdays. The tours take about 45 minutes and begin at different times, depending on the season of the year. While I was researching this book I was unable to take a tour. They had been postponed because of the Governor's new baby and the need for family privacy. Tours did not resume until after this book went to press.

The Seven Gables Restaurant (1205 West Bay Drive NW, Olympia, WA)

The Seven Gables restaurant received it's name from the series of distinctive roof lines or gables of its roof. The house was built in an architectural style known as Gothic Revival. It incorporates typical Victorian designs but includes gothic style gables and bay windows as well as a spindled porch. George Byron Lane built the house in 1893 and used it as much for political entertaining as a home for himself and his wife Nellie Wood Lane.

George Lane had led an interesting life. He rose from humble beginnings as the son of a carpenter to Civil War soldier, to educational administrator to banker and finally a Mayor. Lane came to Washington from the Midwest and settled in Olympia after serving as chief administrator for the states of Nebraska and Missouri. Lane arrived in Olympia in 1891 and became one of the founders of the Olympia State Bank. He also served as mayor of Olympia. While he was mayor he built his fine home. Many political and financial decisions were made over cigars and brandy in front of the massive fireplace in the parlor. After serving as mayor, Lane moved to Seattle, where he died in 1901.

Other prominent residents of the house were the Helenius family. Karl Helenius lived there from from 1912 to 1930. Some people believe that Karl stays on today as a ghost. After Karl's death and sale of the house, the building was put to many uses. It was once a boarding house, an alcohol treatment center and finally became a restaurant and private reception facility. There have been several additions made to the house over the years, but that does not deter the ghost.

The previous owners of the Seven Gables used to let their employees stay overnight in the building. One evening a waitress stayed overnight with her husband. They made sure that they were alone in the building before they went to bed. They made love in the privacy of the second floor bedroom. They were both drifting off when they heard a man's voice by the doorway. It said two words, "Thank you!"

The voice was so unexpected that it frightened them. The possible meaning behind the words was so amusing though, that they were not sure whether to run away or laugh. A voyeuristic ghost is that last thing that either expected in a haunted house. Even though they stayed until morning they never stayed overnight there again.

In 1994 Stephen Taylor and his wife Glennda McLucas-Taylor bought the restaurant and began renovating some of the rooms. Glennda decided to remove some shelving that covered up the large mirror behind the bar. The day after removing the shelves she returned to the lounge and looked at the mirror in the daylight. She saw a stain on the mirror, like someone had removed all of the reflective silvering on the mirror. This stain was in the shape of a perfect heart. Glennda thought that this stain could have been something on the outside of the glass. She began cleaning it, to wipe away whatever was obscuring the glass. It did not work. She cleaned it several times a day. Nothing helped. Then one day the heart was gone.

At the same time as this was happening, Stephen had problems of his own. He installed new carpeting in the hallway between the kitchen and door to the basement stairs. The new carpeting was thicker than the older one. It was so high that the basement door would not open properly. He spent several hours planing down the door. Finally he got it short enough so that it would not stick on the carpeting. A few hours later he returned, opened the door and found that now, for some reason the door was now too wide and would not close properly.

The basement seems to be another focus of paranormal activity. Both Glennda and Stephen have felt a presence there. When they are alone in the building they sometimes hear the sound of voices or footsteps coming from the stairwell. The previous owner told Glennda that the ghost of a little girl has been seen in the back of the basement several times. Up to this point they have not seen her. Nor have they heard the voice of the man, who everyone believes is Karl Helenius. Then again, they do not stay there overnight either.

The Seven Gables is now open only for private parties and receptions. So it will not do for would-be ghost hunters to show up for dinner and ghost story without a reservation.

Port Townsend, Washington

Captain George Vancouver named a little harbor at the tip of the Puget Sound Port Townshend, after his patron, the Marquis of Townshend. The name was later changed to Port Townsend. Settlement of Port Townsend officially began in April of 1851. It was also known as the City of Dreams, because it's settlers' felt that their town would become one of the largest ports on the West Coast. Early capitalists quickly invested money in manufacturing and port facilities. City streets lined with ornate Victorian houses.

Like many other towns and cities of the 19th century, they were too hopeful. The railroads did not build terminals in Port Townsend. Other Puget Sound cities like Seattle and Tacoma were able to out-compete her for their share of the merchant trade. Port Townsend became a quiet backwater. Fortunately for the historic preservation community, the "urban renewal" movement that has destroyed many historic buildings in other Puget Sound communities did not destroy Port Townsend's original buildings.

Manresa Castle

The Manresa Castle hotel reminds many people of the castles that dot the hillsides of Germany's Rhine River valley. The hotel's history explains the similarities in design. It was built by Charles Eisenbeis, a German emigrant and the local industrialist. Perhaps because it reminded him of home. He owned the local brewery, bakery, hotel as well as lumber and brick mills. In 1878 Port Townsend became an incorporated city and Eisenbeis was elected mayor. That is when the Eisenbeis's began construction on their dream home. Their brick kilns and lumber mill supplied the basic building materials for the house's 12 inch thick walls. They brought in skilled woodworkers and artisans who finished the house with imported tile and ornately carved wood trim. After years of work the 30-room house known as the Eisenbeis Castle was completed in

1892.

The Eisenbeis's did not enjoy their home for very long. Charles died in 1902. Kate, who was much younger than Charles soon remarried and moved away. This left the Castle vacant for nearly two decades. In 1925 the house was purchased as a retreat for nuns who taught school in Seattle. In 1927 the house was sold to Jesuit priests who used it as a seminary. In 1928 the Jesuits added a wing to the house that included a chapel and dormitory rooms. They covered the red brick with white stucco and changed the name of the building to Manresa Hall. Manresa is the town in Spain where Ignatius Loyola found their order in the 16th century.

The Jesuits used the building until 1968, when they sold it to investors who converted the building in a hotel. It has changed hands three times since then and each succeeding owner has tried to upgrade the hotel at the same time they have maintained its 19th Century charm.

According to legend, a young Jesuit priest hung himself in the attic above room 302, in the large round tower. This may be the malevolent ghost that appeared to the family that stays in the tower on Halloween to conduct seances. This may be the ghost that appeared as a translucent figure in room 306 and vanished, leaving behind a rotting stench. Footsteps have also been heard in the round tower. The footsteps may be those of a second ghost, named Kate.

Kate was a young Englishwoman who was staying at Manresa when the Eisenbeis family owned it. She was waiting for her fiancé to arrive by ship. After a long waiting period she learned that her lover had died at sea. She was so despondent that she flung herself from one of the tower room windows. She has been seen and heard by numerous people, including a family who regularly conduct seances in the third floor of the tower.

Although several paranormal investigators have visited Manresa Castle and found nothing supernatural, the stories survive. There have been cases where wine glasses have spontaneously shattered in people's hands. Maids cleaning rooms 302 and 306 have heard their names called by disembodied voices and footsteps are still heard by visitors late at night.

Several people have investigated these ghosts. According to the Jefferson County records, there are no reports of a priest committing suicide at Manresa. Descendents of the Eisenbeis family deny any stories about suicide when their family owned the hotel. Some people have countered that the suicides may have been covered up, since suicide is a mortal sin. Investigators have pointed out that the woman who saw the apparition was not wearing her very thick glasses, so she may not have been able to see anything with clarity. Many local people can also attest to a rotting stench coming at nightly intervals from the local paper pulp mill.

Renton, Washington

The Blue Lady

When she was a child, Anna lived with her Aunt and family in a suburban housing development just outside of Renton. She and the rest of the neighborhood children used to play in a small, circular wooded area surrounded by several neighborhood houses. It seemed wild to the children at the time, but the lot was probably only an acre or two in size.

Anna and her cousin Karen used to spend a lot of time walking the trails through "woods", building tree forts or playing on the rope swing someone had hung from a maple tree. One afternoon as they were walking to their favorite spot, Karen stopped and grabbed Anna's arm. She asked Anna if she heard a woman calling their names. Anna did not hear anything, but Karen insisted she heard a woman's voice. Anna suggested it was her aunt calling the two girls. Karen maintained that it was not her mother, Anna's aunt. They continued arguing all the way to the swing.

They forgot all about the voice calling them as they took

turns on the swing. Anna went first, then Karen. Anna was pushing her when Karen screamed, let go of the rope and jumped off of the swing. Karen pointed at bushes surrounding the tree and swing. Anna saw a woman with glowing white skin and a long blue dress standing at the edge of the bushes. The woman raised her arm and pointed a finger at the two girls. They were paralyzed with fear as the woman began walking toward them. She reached out to the girls with an open hand. Karen screamed. That seemed to release them. The girls ran to their house without looking back.

Many elements of this story are fairly common such as children playing in the woods, ghostly voices calling them and a mysterious lady. The thing that is interesting to me is the setting. One of the things fairly common in post World War II urban planning is the cul-de-sac. The road into the housing development ends in a big circle and the houses are built around the paved circle. In Anna's neighborhood, the houses were built around a vacant lot. Was the lot always vacant? What if the house she lived in was built around an older structure that was destroyed by the time Anna moved in? Could the maple tree have been planted years earlier as landscaping for a large house or graveyard? We'll never know.

Seattle, Washington

She doesn't live here anymore? (Private Residence, Seattle, WA)

In the early 1990s "Jane" and her boyfriend moved into a small one room cottage in south Seattle. It was part of a complex of retirement homes that had been opened up for general tenants in the last few years. The place was in a less than savory part of town but the rent was cheap and they were allowed to plant their own flower garden in front of the cottage.

Shortly after they moved in they noticed a cat hanging around their new home and they let it come in. The cat acted as if it had been there before. It even had a favorite place to lie down. Soon after they started letting the cat into the house, they noticed a faint moaning sound. It sounded like a woman's voice. Jane and her boyfriend thought that it was just the neighbors. They were too embarrassed to go next door and ask them to keep the noise down. The neighbors moved and the moaning continued. If anything it was even louder.

They began looking for a different cause. It was not the plumbing, a draft or other mundane causes. They noticed that their furniture had begun to move. Sometimes Jane thought that she saw chairs move a bit, but could not be sure. They drew circles around the legs of chairs. After a few minutes they would check to see if anything happened. In many cases the furniture had moved outside of the circles. At the height of the haunting activity they even saw a visual manifestation. Both Jane and her boyfriend saw what looked like a glowing white rope. It seemed to float and dance around the little cottage.

It was just before these sightings that they had a clue as to the identity of the moaning woman. Jane's boyfriend found that their new cat had been in a fight. Its paw had been badly mauled. He held it in his lap and examined the injured leg. The cat began squirming in his lap and meowed to be let down. At that moment the moaning began from the back of the apartment grew louder.

"NO!" came the sound of a woman's voice.

Several items in the bathroom were knocked off of their shelves and a large beach towel flew from the bathroom into the kitchen. He let go of the cat, which jumped down. The moaning stopped. This convinced them that the cat was associated with the cottage and a former tenant. Jane talked with a neighbor who had lived in the complex for some time. An old lady had been a tenant in their little bungalow. She had kept eight cats there for quite some time. One day the little old lady was gone. Jane's informant did not know if the old woman had died or been moved to a permanent care facility. The management had cleared out the cottage and turned out the cats in the process. Jane's new cat had been the only one to stay around the area.

They continued to live in the same little cottage for a few more months. Although the thought of sharing a house with a ghost frightened them, it was also exciting. The sounds gradually faded away. Jane guessed that the cat's former owner was satisfied that her pet was being taken care of and had decided to move on.

Metro Ghost (Metro Transit's South Operations Base, Seattle, Washington)

For many years there have been rumors and stories that the facility used by Seattle's Metro for their southern operations is haunted. Many of the sightings and strange incidents have been reported in the evenings or early mornings. Workers have reported experiencing cold spots, hearing knocks, seeing objects moving and falling off shelves in front of their eyes.

Security guards and maintenance personnel are usually the most open and honest people when talking about paranormal experiences in the buildings where they work. The Stanley Smith Company runs security for the facility. According to Pat Kelly, the personnel manager for Stanley Smith, several of their guards refuse to work the night shift at Metro. One nighttime guard, Ingrid Carroher reported seeing a man dressed in brown clothing. Minutes after she spotted the man, he vanished without a trace.

It is possible that the ghost haunting the facility is not a former employee. Like many large organizations, Metro has it's own internal newsletter. According to one newsletter, before the facility was built the land was used as a quarry site. One of the workers was named Robin. He was killed in a horrible accident. Since the article was published, workers at the facility have named the ghost Robin.

The Underground Guard (Seattle Underground Tour, Seattle, WA)

The Seattle Underground is in reality the basement or ground floor levels of the buildings of the original Seattle. Shortly after Seattle was founded, the streets of Seattle were built up several feet above ground level. The building entrances and sidewalks were several feet lower, at the original ground level. Several years later sidewalks were constructed on the same level as the built-up streets. This turned the ground floor shops and office buildings into basements and the 2nd or 3rd floors into ground level entrances.

In the 1970s a *Kolchak the Night Stalker* movie had a century old Jack-the-Ripper type killer hiding under multiple levels of forgotten construction. Even before that movie, the mention of the Seattle Underground evoked a feeling of depression among some people who took the underground tour. Although the tour guides are witty and well informed and many of the stories have a humorous twist, when you walk through the underground, you are literally walking back in time. It can be a dark and musty trip with water dripping in dimly lit corridors, experiencing in part, some of the scenes of the past.

This includes businesses that failed, breaking hearts, stories of poisonings, drownings and other incidents of mayhem that happened when Seattle was young. Most tour groups seem to stir up something alarming, like the random, skulking rat. A smaller number of tour groups may have stirred up ghosts as well.

It is easy to imagine ghosts anywhere in the dark corridors of the underground. Many people have seen a figure standing in the basement of a building that was once a bank. Some people have speculated that the figure was that of a man, standing next to the old bank's vault. This apparition has been interpreted to be an old-time bank guard who for some reason still keeps vigil over his century old guard post.

Skykomish

The Skykomish Hotel (102 Railroad Avenue East, Skykomish, Washington)

John Stevens founded Skykomish in 1889. It was originally named Maloney's Siding but it was later changed to Skykomish, a Native American name that translates as *Inland People*. In the 1920s, the population of Skykomish was 8,000. Today it has around 270 year round residents. For Skykomish the end of the timber mill was the final straw after the old sawmill, cement plant and railroad left the town. The city is now trying to recover and rebuild the town by attracting skiers in winter and hikers in summer. Many people from the larger cities have summer homes in the pass

One of the tourist attractions and facilities of the town is the Skykomish hotel. It's appeal is in its location in the west end of Steven's Pass and it's ghost. The Skykomish Hotel was built in 1904 and has 28 rooms. Like many rough and ready towns of the Pacific Northwest in the 19th and early 20th Centuries, not all of the hotel residents had employment outside of their rooms. In the 1920s, a prostitute named Mary was murdered in Room 32 by one of her customers.

Don Flynn bought the old hotel in 1990. He claims to have seen Mary's ghost once and felt her presence several more times. One day he and an assistant were making repairs to a bathroom fixture on the third floor. He saw the apparition of a woman in a white negligee walk or glide by the bathroom. On two occasions he felt her presence. Once she followed him down the stairs. On a different occasion he watched the door to room 32 unlock, open and the lights came on. Again, he did not see anyone.

Flynn admitted that some people have exaggerated stories of Mary's appearances in the hopes of increasing tourism. He would no longer benefit from this either. Flynn recently sold the hotel to the Steven's Pass Company, who used it as housing for their winter personnel. The haunting still continue though. I spoke with Laurie, a hotel employee. She and other people have felt cold spots when walking down an otherwise warm hallway. Several people have heard voices talking in and around the third floor bathrooms, which may have been Mary's room.

The haunting extends from the third floor rooms down into the café attached to the hotel lobby. One morning one of the new cooks heard the familiar sound of someone eating in one of the middle booths. He heard a knife and fork scraping and cutting against a plate and the clank as silverware was put down on the countertop. The only problem was that he had not started cooking and the café was empty. He told Laurie his story and she confirmed that she had heard ghostly eating herself more than once.

The hotel is open in the summer for their regular clientele of tourists and travelers. It may be open for regular business next winter; the employees were a little too rowdy last winter and the Company may not house them next year.

Skykomish Railroad Ghosts (Skykomish, Washington)

A few miles farther up Steven's pass from Skykomish are the remains of the town of Wellington. This is the site of the Wellington train disaster of 1910. That February, snow banks west of the old pass tunnel stalled two westbound trains. The trains were delayed overnight as work crews tried to clear the tracks.

On March 1st an avalanche swept down the mountainside, carrying both trains over a hundred feet to the bottom of the river valley. Ninety-six people were killed in the disaster. The remains of the trains can still be seen in the valley floor. This disaster may account for the rumors of ghost trains, the sounds of crashes and the screams of people echoing through the passes in winter evenings.

The Great Northern changed the name of the *Wellington* to *Tye* to disassociate it from the disaster. A few year later the Great Northern moved the operations from Tye to Skykomish and the little community of Tye faded away. The old town site can be reached along the Iron Goat Trail, a new interpretive trail constructed along the old train route. The trail is wheel chair accessible and ends at the old town site.

Steilacoom, WA

The town of Steilacoom was the first incorporated town in the Puget Sound in 1854. Lafayette Balch, a sea captain from Maine outfitted two ships with all of the supplies necessary to begin a small town, including finished lumber and supplies for houses and a general store. Balch named his new settlement Port Steilacoom. A few months later John Chapman arrived and located his Donation Land Claim south of Balch's. He called his new settlement Steilacoom City. Trying to establish two towns so close together was foolish and both men compromised. They decided that the town would be cited on the land where the two land claims joined together. It was named simply Steilacoom. Steilacoom's main street was named Union Avenue.

By 1855, 70 houses, three hotels and several stores and shops were built on and near Union Avenue. Nearby manufacturing included three sawmills, a slaughterhouse and a gristmill. Other social institutions included a school, a billiard hall and bowling alley. For many years industry in Steilacoom thrived until the railroads settled in nearby towns like Tacoma and Seattle and development bypassed Steilacoom.

Like many older communities in the Pacific Northwest, there were many dreamers who came west to seek their fortunes. Some of these people succeeded in making their dreams come true. Other people's dreams did not come true. Steilacoom in particular may be populated by some of the dreamers like Albert Balch and J.M. Bates, who may walk the city streets at night.

Albert Balch, lunatic? (Albert Balch house, Steilacoom, WA)

Steilacoom's founder, Lafayette Balch helped build a house for his brother Albert in 1857. Albert's house is a good example of the early architecture of the time. The beams still have the original adz marks from the rough shaping tools used. Lafayette hired Albert, a bachelor as the storekeeper of the original town store, which Lafayette had also built. Albert Balch was a respected citizen; most of the time. He even served on the jury of a local murder trial, despite his suffering from periodic lunacy.

The term lunacy has been dropped from the current list of psychological illnesses, which are now very definitive. A person with lunacy suffers from short periods of mental impairment divided by periods of normal mental activity. It was called lunacy because people used to think that this form of mental illness was tied to the phases of the moon. Albert Balch seems to have been a true lunatic.

He would act strangely whenever there was a new moon. He would seem to lose focus, often walking around at night, looking at the sky. He would disappear for days, only to return as if nothing happened, after the moon changed it's cycle. Most of the time Albert Balch would wander around in a daze, not knowing who he was or what he was doing. In the beginning he was not violent, just highly confused. His condition became worse as time went on. The Balch family sent him to an asylum in San Francisco where he seemed to recover his mental faculties. After the cure Albert returned to Steilacoom.

He arrived home in time to once again have a relapse. In 1859 Albert was sent to San Francisco to buy merchandise for the store. He suffered one of his spells. A brother who lived there eventually found him wandering the streets with $2,500 in gold coins in his valise. The Balch family tried various different cures that did not work. His lunacy became more severe and many local townspeople began to fear him.

Whether it was a sign of his dementia or the changing attitude of the local townspeople, Albert Balch become convinced that he had enemies who were trying to kill him. In late December of 1862 the new moon was too hard for Albert to resist. On the night of the 27th, he ran out of his house dressed in his nightshirt. His body was found on the trail to Fort Nisqually. The official coroner's inquest determined that Balch had been running from his house to escape from his imaginary pursuers and had either fallen and killed himself or had run until he collapsed from exhaustion and died of exposure.

He may still wander the trail on the night of the new moon or he may be an unseen presence that presides over his old home, again. It was moved to its present location a century ago. Unfortunately, this move damaged the house's fireplaces and chimney. The house was restored in 1995, which may have pleased Albert Balch's spirit.

E.R. Rogers Restaurant and Haunted House (1702 Commercial St, Steilacoom, WA)

Merchant Captain E.R. Rogers built his Mansion around 1891 for himself, his wife Catherine and their daughter. Like many who made their living by the sea, Rogers lost his fortune in 1893 and had to sell his house. It was purchased by Charles Herman, who renamed it the Waverly Inn. His guests were treated to a wood stove in every room and an indoor bath on each floor. These were luxurious accommodations for those times. W.L. and Hattie Bair purchased the property in 1920.

They lived there and operated it as a boarding house for many years.

Popular legend has it that E.R. Rogers and perhaps some members of his family have returned after death to their dream home. Some people claim to have seen Rogers sitting in a rocking chair, looking out of a north-facing window. That particular chair is usually found placed under that window. Even if it had been put in a nearby closet the night before. In October of 1996, the late Jack Sage was on the first floor of the restaurant talking about it's past to a large audience when the ghosts made themselves felt, or rather heard. From the vacant upstairs Sage and his audience heard a series of heavy thumps above their heads.

In October of 1997 the restaurant bookkeeper Kristi, was working near the bar in the restaurant. It was morning and she was trying to concentrate on her paperwork but she had trouble because of the noise from the bell at the end of the bar. It rang, for several minutes. She attributed the ringing to a draft and did not get up to investigate. She mentioned this to the owner who informed her that there was no draft near the bar. Patrons and employees have had strange experiences in the restaurant, particularly the attic.

One bar patron was having a drink and nearly choked when he saw the stockinged foot of a woman appear in the air above him. He watched the foot and presumably leg it was attached to walking up and through the ceiling into the attic above him. Unknown to the bar patron, before the house was converted into a restaurant there had been a flight of stairs leading to the second floor where he had seen the woman's foot disappear. Apparently the ghost didn't know that the stair had been removed.

Jennifer Laughlin was an employee at E.R. Rogers in the 1980s. She went into the attic for some spare chairs. While she was searching the attic she began to smell cheap perfume. In a few minutes its scent became overpowering. She did not see anyone in the attic with her, but she felt a presence that made her feel uneasy. Even animals avoid the attic.

One night the last employee to leave the building saw lights on inside when he had turned them off. He called the police, who arrived with a canine unit. The police sent the dog into each room to clear the house before entering. The dog entered each room without finding anything unusual. Except the attic. The dog refused to climb the final stairs and enter. The police had to check it themselves without the dog. They found the attic empty.

There are other stories and folklore surrounding a Native American who may have been hung on or near the house site. His apparition is sometimes seen in the yard or looking in through the windows. Many people have heard sounds of footsteps in empty rooms and felt chills and strange sounds.

Some people have suggested that Mrs. Bair may be one of the spirits haunting the house she presided over for so many years. I spoke with a member of the Steilacoom historical society who denied the validity of any stories of hauntings there. She visited the house several times as a child when the Bairs were in residence. She told me that Mrs. Bair ran a respectable house and would have been scandalized at the thought of ghosts in her house, much less becoming one of its ghosts.

Does J.M. Bates walk the streets of Steilacoom ? (Steilacoom, WA)

In the 1850s Steilacoom was a thriving metropolis. It had successful entrepreneurs like Andrew Byrd, who owned a sawmill, gristmill and slaughterhouse. It also had its share of not-so-successful citizens such as J.M. Bates whose main asset was a lone cow. He was quite proud of it. One day the cow came up missing.

Bates went looking for his prized animal. He stopped at one of the many saloons that used to line Steilacoom's main street. One of the bar patrons, told Bates that he had seen Andrew Byrd taking the cow to the slaughterhouse. Bates was incensed and went looking for Byrd. He found him in the Post

Office. After a brief exchange, in which Byrd denied having anything to do with the missing cow, Bates shot him.

Byrd did not die immediately. He urged the bystanders and sheriff not to hurt or prosecute Bates. Byrd died the next day and Bates was put in jail. That night a group of decided to take matters into their own hands. They broke into the jail and locked the sheriff up in one of his own cells. They took Bates into a nearby barn and hung him. The man who told Bates that Byrd had stolen his cow left town. Bates still remains. According to some, Bates has been seen on dark nights, still wearing his hangman's noose; looking for his lost cow.

Tacoma, WA

Babysitter ghost (Private Residence in Tacoma, Washington)

In January of 1990 Catherine and her husband bought a 15 year old ranch style house just outside of Tacoma. It was their first house and they were on a budget because they were expecting their first child. A few months later their son was born. Shortly afterward Catherine began to felt uncomfortably when she was alone in the living room. She spoke with her husband about this and he admitted feeling the same himself. Some time passed and the feeling continued.

When her son began to walk she noticed he behaved strangely in the living room. Her baby liked to "patrol" the house after he learned to walk. He would wake Catherine up in the middle of the night and the two of them would go for walks through the house together. He would lean against her to let her know where he wanted to go. Each time he woke Catherine up, she would stop outside each room, hoping that he would go in. He bypassed these rooms in favor of a trip straight to the living room. Once he peeked into the living room his curiosity seemed to be satisfied and he was content to have mommy take him back to his room for a feeding before going to sleep.

This went on for several months. The feeling never got

any stronger, but it did not go away either. She tried various methods to relieve the strange sensation. A friend gave her a quartz ball that was supposed to absorb negative energy. Catherine tried making an old folk cure, called a witch bottle to do the same thing. Neither appeared to be completely successful. After several months the feeling gradually faded away. Catherine believed that the presence, whatever it was just got used to them. She was able to stay in the living room until late, although she hurried out of the room when the lights were turned off.

The presence returned when they made arrangements to sell their house in 1996. Initially they were going to sell it to a couple with children. This sale did not happen. The next prospective buyer was a single man with no children. As they were negotiating the sale, the presence came back. They could tell it was not happy. Someone had told Catherine that an older couple had lived in the house before Catherine purchased it. They felt that the presence had not only come to tolerate them but like them and their son. Catherine felt that it was possible that they were still around and that they prefered the house alive with children.

The McCormick-Wheelock Library (3722 N 26th St, Tacoma, WA)

The North McCormick-Wheelock library was originally named the McCormick library, after Anna McCormick; whose family were benefactors of the local library system. In late 1995 it was decided to change the name of the library to include the name of Anna Wheelock, after her daughter bequeathed $2.4 million dollars to the library for the change. This took effect in the early months of 1996.

Mike Sarach and his family owned their own janitorial business. One of their contracts was to clean the nine Tacoma City library branches in 1995. The regular cleaning crew consisted of the Sarachs and their grown children. In October of 1995 Mike read the proposed name change announcement out loud to his family while they were cleaning the North End McCormick-Wheelock branch. Shortly after that strange things began to happen.

One night Sarach's daughter Janelle, had just finished cleaning the building. As she left the library and walked to her car she looked through a window and saw several boxes in a storage room fall to the floor. A few evenings later Mike was cleaning the staff restroom. After cleaning, Mike unplugged the space heater and left the restroom. Shortly afterward he heard the sound of running water coming from the room he had just left. He ran back into the restroom and found the water had been turned on and the heater was plugged in again.

That same evening Mike's wife, Donna heard someone calling her name. Donna was standing by the library's front counter when she heard the voice. It sounded like a woman's soft whisper. Donna is blind and could not see who called her. At first she thought that it was one of her daughters but soon found out that she was standing alone at the front counter. There were other strange incidents over a three-week period.

Another daughter, Ann watched a bar-type swinging hinge door begin to swing on its own for several seconds. On another night Mike Sarach dropped a cleaning cloth on the floor. Before he could bend down to pick it up, the towel rose up on it's own and floated over to him. Sarach was certainly surprised but felt that it was just the ghost trying to be helpful.

Janelle had another encounter that gave the Sarach's some clue as to the identity of the ghost. Janelle was in the back room of the library emptying a garbage can. Out of the corner of her eye she saw a figure at the circulation desk. Janelle saw a solid seeming apparition of a woman in her late sixties. The woman was grey haired and full figured. The woman turned and looked at Janelle and smiled at her. She turned to face the older woman, who then vanished.

These incidents happened over a three-week period and then abruptly ended. Since that time neither the daytime employees nor the cleaning staff, or reporter C.R. Roberts who stayed for a late night vigil have seen or heard anything unusual. The Sarach's, felt that the ghost was either Anna McCormick who was making her presence known (in protest of the name change) or Anna Wheelock, who was moving into the building that would soon bear her name.

I visited the library in 1999. I spoke with the two librarians who were on duty. When I asked if they had heard anything about the hauntings they rolled their eyes a little bit and told me that they had been asked the same question several times. They had not had seen or heard anything strange happen in the library. They also told me that if there were a ghost they would not be afraid since both Mrs. Wheelock and Mrs. McCormick loved libraries and would not hurt anyone.

The Pierce County Courthouse (Tacoma, WA)

The Pierce County courthouse was opened in June of 1893. Like many municipal buildings built in those days, local governments wanted to build something to contrast the local stick and timber frame building that made up most of the local buildings. The Courthouse has four above ground floors and a high ceiling attic on the 5th floor. Some of the interesting feature of the courthouse included a secret stairway for conducting prisoners from the jail to the judge's chambers on the third floor. This was done to quietly conduct dangerous or controversial prisoners to the courtroom; and allow the judge to leave discreetly.

Before the State prison in Walla Walla was constructed, executions were conducted at the local level. That meant that the Pierce County Sheriff was responsible for conducting executions of condemned prisoners. Toward the turn of the century the dubious festival surrounding public hangings ended. Instead, a high platform with 13 steps was erected in room 506, in the courthouse attic as the County gallows. Years later the Washington State Prison with its death house was constructed and prisoners were sent there for execution.

As time passed and Pierce County continued to grow,

records accumulated and were stored in the attic. Despite this change in usage, employees still told stories of strange happenings in the attic. These stories grew in the telling, adding more people and horrific crimes attributed to them. Fortunately, records have been kept as to the number of people executed and their crimes. There were only two.

One executed murderer was Albert Michaud. He was executed on the 6th of April, 1900 at 7:10AM. Michaud was a French-Canadian, who murdered Mrs. John Amber and then tried to commit suicide. Michaud was so frightened of being hanged that his black hair turned snowy white by the time of his execution. The Sheriff at that time was a man named Mills. To ensure that he did the job properly he went to Spokane to learn execution techniques by watching a hanging there. Although Michaud's hanging was not as public as if done in the city square, 80 people watched.

The second person hung in room 509 was a man named Eben Boyce. Boyce had served in the United State's Army during the Manila campaign at the end of the 19th Century. By 1900 he had returned to the United States, where he earned a poor living as a traveling museum roustabout. Boyce's wife had left him during this period but he tracked her down. On the 10th of February, he entered the restaurant where she worked, drew a pistol and shot her. He was convicted of murder and hanged on the 9th of August 1901. On the day of his execution Boyce nearly collapsed on the walk up to the scaffold.

According to the County employees of the past and later residents of the building there are strange noises in the attic of the old courthouse. Reported sounds include heavy footsteps, loud thumps and the sound of choking or gasping. Could this have been the sound of the two condemned men reenacting their executions? The old building has been replaced or upgraded now. Have these changes released the ghosts, or do they remain?

The Old Tacoma City Hall (625 Commerce St, Tacoma, WA)

Many of the security guards who had to patrol the wide hallways have seen and complained of fleeting shadows walking around them. One night in February of 1979 the police were summoned repeatedly to the old building when burglar and fire alarms went off several times. When they arrived each time the building was secured and there were not trespassers on the premises. The police and guards within the building did note some strange events.

Lights would flick on in one room and then off and then turn on in other rooms. It was as if someone were hurrying through the building playing with the light switches. The guards hurried through the building trying to catch the intruder or intruders. Despite their efforts they never saw anyone.

Many Tacoma residents are familiar with the old courthouses bell tower. Within the tower there were four 60-pound bells, which are gone now. Mr. and Mrs. Hugh Wallace, former US Ambassador donated these bells in memory of their daughter who had died at the tragically young age of 12. There were no ropes attached to the bells to cause them to be rung. The bell clappers were connected to the tower clock by a series of rods that caused them to ring on the hour. These were disconnected, leaving no way to cause the bells to ring without someone being in the tower and physically moving the clappers manually. Despite this fact the bells in the tower were rung repeatedly in the past.

Guards have noticed that the lights in the bell tower, which should have been left on had been turned off. Then sometime during the night they would hear the bells toll. When they investigated the tower was empty. No matter how quickly they reached the tower, they did not meet anyone on the stairs up to the bell chamber. One evening the building manager Jim Brewster spent the evening in the bell tower. Although he did not see anyone or hear the bells toll, he felt a presence in the tower that convinced him that there was a ghost in the tower.

The Old City Hall has been converted into upscale businesses as diverse as architects and aromatherapy. A large portion of the ground floor has been turned into the T.B. & G., the Tacoma Bar & Grill. In 1999 I visited the T.B. & G. and spoke with owner Stephanie Clark and Claude, one of the employees. According to them the ghost or ghosts are still active.

According to lore handed down from maintenance and security staff, the basement had a series of temporary holding cells for prisoners. Claude escorted me to what may have been a solitary confinement cell. Stephanie stayed in the restaurant; she never goes down to the basement. When she does, she frequently hears spiritual screams. Claude showed me the basement. Hidden in a small back closet is a metal-framed door with a small sliding metal panel located at eye height. This door opens into a small three foot by three foot room. I cannot think of any use for this room other than as a cell. Claude showed me another small room that may have been cell. Hetold me that several people have seen the figure of a man walking around in the basement. He is usually seen entering or leaving this room.

This ghost may be the same one who inhabits T.B. & G.'s upstairs. This ghost is known as Gus. He seems to be harmless and engages in the occasional poltergeist prank. During the grand opening of the bar they were cooking lunch for a full house when the stove stopped working. There was nothing wrong with the electricity or the stove. It just stopped working. It started working again as soon as lunch was over. On one occasion Claude was walking from the bar into the back lounge when all of the wine glasses resting on a sideboard shattered. It may have been Gus's way of letting Claude know who was boss. Most of the employees experienced something like this shortly after coming to work.

On two occasions Stephanie was observing two new bartenders on their first night there. Shortly after their shift started, they all watched in amazement as all of the bottles tumbled off of their shelves, one by one. It was as if someone walked along behind the bar, knocking them down with a finger. Strangely enough, none of the bottle broke. Most of the employees have had something like this happen. A few people have been pestered and left. The best way to stop it is to come to terms with Gus. Stephanie told me; "Everyone talks to Gus!"

Whidbey Island

Haunted Photo Lab (Whidbey Island Naval Air Station Fleet Imaging Center, Building 243)

Like many military bases, Whidbey Island Naval Air Station has several buildings of different ages that have served many purposes over the years. Building 243 was constructed in 1945 as a 28 bed dispensary, or medical clinic. In addition to patient wards, it included a pharmacy, small laboratory and operating room. Like many hospitals and clinics, this one seems to have left some former patients behind when it was converted into a Fleet Imaging Center. The "Fleet Imaging Center" is a high tech photography and film lab for processing and audio-visual projects within the base. The building has been used for this purpose since the 1970s. In the last nearly 30 years there have been many stories about strange noises and incidents in the building.

In the spring of 1995 Roberto Taylor witnessed a

stranger than usual series of incidents. On this particular evening Taylor received a phone call from one of the Base's security guards. The guard had seen a light on in one of the building offices. While the guard was watching the window he saw someone move the blinds open slightly and look out at him. Taylor was the duty photographer for the night and had the keys to all of the locked doors in the building. He came immediately.

He and the guard entered the building and began searching from room to room. All of the rooms were empty. They came to the room where the lights had been on, but it was now off. They unlocked the door and the guard pushed his guard dog into the room. After a few seconds the dog came running out. The frustrated guard forced his dog into the office again. The dog immediately ran out again. This time it hid behind the guard! The two men opened the door and turned on the light. The room was empty.

Jody Lanham has worked late in the evening several times. He has heard strange noises that were not the result of the building settling. One night he was working in the building storeroom. He heard someone open the door leading from the front office and reception room and walk down the hallway leading to the other offices. Lanham knew he was alone in the building so he quickly left his work to investigate. He opened the store room door and found that the hallway empty. There had been no sounds of doors opening or closing, as if someone hidden in one of the offices.

Anthony Smith does not stay in the building after dark if he can help it. He has heard footsteps and strange noises in various parts of the building. At one time he was one of three people who had keys to the building. One morning it was his responsibility open the building before the rest of the sailors arrived for duty. He was the last one out the night before. That night he made sure that all of the office equipment was turned off as well as the coffee machine, radios, etc. When he unlocked the doors at 6:45 in the morning he heard the sound of a radio playing. It was not hard to find, since it was playing with the volume turned on full blast.

Smith was often the first person in the building in the morning. Several times he has found office lights turned on, when he knew that he had turned them off the night before. He once found a computer turned on, but a photocopy machine plugged into the same power strip was still turned off. Now and then if he is lucky (or unlucky), he has heard voices talking. He cannot make out what the voices are saying, they are too muffled. Like Lanham, he has also heard the sound of footsteps when he is alone in the building.

I received this story from Tony Popp, a journalist with the base newspaper, the *Crosswind*. He has worked in and out of the building for some time. He has not been able to find out how many people have died in the building when it was the infirmary or a possible identity of the ghost or ghosts, but he and the others are believers that there is something not quite normal in Building 243.

It Began with a Scratching (Private residence on Whidbey Island)

Several years ago Lynn Dublin and her husband Frank moved into a small farmhouse on Whidbey Island. It was quite a drive for Frank, who was stationed at Ft Lewis. But the price was right and they didn't mind the isolation. Their mailbox was located a mile away, up their driveway.

Shortly after they settled in Lynn and Frank began hearing a scratching sound from under their living room floor. At first they thought it was mice or small animals living under the floorboards. They were living in the country and small pests are part of experience. Shortly after the scratching began, they began experiencing things that would be difficult for mice to cause.

One day they watched the doorknob on the back door begin to turn. They were startled because they had not heard anyone walk up to the back porch. Frank walked to the door and opened it. There was no one there. The knob had still been turning when Frank grabbed the knob and finished opening it. They did tried and explain it away as some kind of animal outside, resting against the door, turning the knob. A few minutes later they heard a rattling sound and rushed to the front door.

They watched the knob turn back and forth several times. Once again, when the door was opened, no one was there. This happened several times, and each time Frank or Lynn opened the door there was no one there. They tried to ignore the phenomenon. In most hauntings this tactic usually works. The ghost-hosters get used to the phenomenon and get on with their lives. After a while they do not even notice. Sometimes the phenomenon fades away, as if it took on energy from the anxiety of the homeowners. Unfortunately, this did not work for the Dublins. In addition to the scratching and rattling door knobs there were more noises.

Many evenings the windows would rattle, as if they were being hit by a heavy wind. Whidbey Island experiences many heavy winds from the Puget Sound. Rattling windows are a part of life, except this sometimes happened on calm nights. They both began to hear music coming from the attic, as if a band was playing there. After six months the Dublins moved into a quieter house in town. Their ex-landlord admitted to them that there was a rumor that the farmhouse was built on top of an old Indian burial ground.

Works Consulted

Books

Bingham, Joan and Dolores Riccio

1991 *More Haunted Houses.* Pocket Books, a division of Simon & Schuster Inc., New York, NY.

Dyer, James C. Jr.

1985 *Historic Houses of Steilacoom*, Proverbial Press, Steilacoom, WA.

Curits, Joan, Watson, Alice & Bette Bradley (ed.)

1988 *Town on the Sound, Stories of Steilacoom*, Steilacoom Historical Museum, Steilacoom, WA.

Periodicals

Anonymous
1 January 1863, "The death of Albert Balch", *Puget Sound Herald*, p.2.

Anonymous
1982 "The strange story of Albert Balch", *Steilacoom Historical Museum Quarterly*, vol. XI, p. 9., Steilacoom, WA.

Anonymous
3 September 1997 "Ghostly tales," *South County Journal*, Tacoma, WA.

Clements Barbara and Gestin Suttle
31 October 1996 They lurk, they stomp, they haunt/many ghosts apparently call Tacoma area home." *The News Tribune,* Tacoma, WA.

Dumas, Paul,
7 April 1959 "Ghost reported half century about county hanging room," *Tacoma News Tribune*, Tacoma, WA.

Ericson, Jim
31 October 1981 "There's a creak and clatter...." *Tacoma News Tribune*, Tacoma, WA.

Godden, Jean
4 August 1991 "Beware the ghost that haunts Metro Base," the *Seattle Times*, p. B1, Seattle, WA.

Happy, Rita
1 September 1994, "Restoring a sense of history," *Tacoma News Tribune 50 plus section*, p.1, Tacoma, WA.

Lane, Bob
18 February 1979, "Ghosts in Tacoma? It's no laughing matter," *Tacoma News Tribune*, Tacoma, WA.

Merryman, Kathleen
31 October 1991, "Historic haunts: along the streets of Steilacoom linger memories and maybe more than that-of dead residents", *Tacoma News Tribune*, Tacoma, WA.

Merryman, Kathleen
30 October 1992 "Historic Haunts", *Tacoma News Tribune*, Tacoma, WA.

Moodie, Neil
24 October 1998 "This town is rich with history and volunteers," *Seattle Post-Intelligencer*, Seattle, WA.

O'Neal, Dori
31 October 1993 "Tales from the crypt", *Tri-City Herald*, Kennewick, WA.

Penny, Ray D.

22 May 1955 "Court house steeped in history of Tacoma," The *Tacoma Sunday Ledger*, Tacoma, WA.

Popp, Tony-

31 October 1997 "Is base photo lab home to ghosts?" *Crosswind*, Whidbey Island Naval Air Station, p. A-6.

Ripp, Bart

7 June 1992 "A magician's favorite haunt: Tacoma's Ray Gamble", *Tacoma News Tribune*, p. D8, Tacoma, WA.

Roberts, R.C.

12 March 1996 "The library ghost who didn't check in...", *Tacoma News Tribune*, Tacoma, WA.

Tewkesbury, Don

29 October 1993 "Eerie apparition drives adults from castle," *Seattle Post Intelligencer*, p. C1-C1, Seattle, Wa.

Internet Resources

Gamaz, Anna

December 1998 "The Blue Lady," *Castle of Spirits web page* at www.rpi.net.au/~ghostgum/castle.

Gordon, Robin

December 1998 "The Everett House," *Castle of Spirits web page* at www.rpi.net.au/~ghostgum/castle.

Mills, Rick

October 1995 "Fort Lewis," *Obiwan's ufo free paranormal web page* at www.ghosts.org.html

Rollosson, Catherine

March 1997 "The Presence," *Obiwan's ufo free paranormal web page* at www.ghosts.org.html

Stromberg, Pierre

September 1997 "My stay at the Manresa Castle," *Pierre Stromberg's Paranomal Northwest* website at www.eskimo.com/~pierres.html

Unknown

March 1995 "Cat Woman," *Obiwan's ufo free paranormal web page* at www.ghosts.org.html

Unknown

October 1995 "Fort Lewis," *Obiwan's ufo free paranormal web page* at www.ghosts.org.html

Unknown

December 1998 "The Old Seattle Ghost", *Stories Far & Near*, www.hauntings.com.

Eastern Washington

Colbert, Washington

Twenty four Days (A private residence in Colbert, Washington)

In the late 1970s the "Heston" family were looking for a new house. There were nine people in the family, from a four month old baby to teenage daughters and two family dogs. They found a place that was large enough for the whole family, if some of the children slept in the basement. In the case of most haunted houses the ghostly phenomenon begins slowly and builds to a climax. In this case, there was no build-up; the Hestons were treated to a near immediate climax. The children in the basement told their parents that pictures flew off of their dressers and the walls. There were no breezes, drafts or earthquakes to account for this. Doors would open and close when no one was there.

Several of the children reported seeing apparitions late at night. One of the teenage daughters woke up and saw an apparition standing over the crib of her four month old brother. She thought she saw a knife in it's hand. She screamed and it vanished. Another daughter saw the apparition on another night. She was so frightened that she fell down and cut her neck trying to escape.

Some of this phenomenon might be blamed on the power of suggestion and anxiety on the part of the children in a new house. What about Mr. Heston? There were several times when he was alone in the house. On these occasions he heard loud bangs echoing throughout the house. It sounded like someone was pounding on the walls with a heavy hammer. This went on for some time before the Heston's called a priest and asked him to bless the house. The priest arrived and performed his ritual. He later stated that he did not feel anything strange or menacing in the house. Despite the exorcism the strange noises and apparitions continued. The Hestons moved out after a 24 day stay in their new home.

Spokane, Washington

The Cloud, (Near the intersection of Garland and Cedar, Spokane, WA)

In 1995 Ryan and his girlfriend Deshan were walking to an all night coffee shop in the Shadle district of Spokane. It was around one in the morning but they were not worried. It was a warm August night and the neighborhood was safe and well lit. When they reached the intersection of Garland and Cedar it ceased being warm, well lit or safe.

As they passed under the lamp post on the southeast corner of the intersection the light went out. Although this was startling, street lights do go out. They continued walking. About four feet away from the street lamp they were hit by a moving pocket of cold air that hit them hard enough to rock them off their heels. The cold air passed them, stopped and began spreading outward, surrounding them. Deshan grabbed Ryan's arm and dragged him away so hard that the next day he had bruises on his arm. After running to the other end of the block they stopped and looked back at the intersection. They saw a pale grey cloud hovering above the ground. It was hard to tell how big it was, considering the distance. Ryan guessed it was about nine foot high and five feet wide. They watched it hover there for several seconds before they headed for the coffee shop.

A few nights later they took the same route toward the coffee shop again. They speculated about what they might encounter but did not know what to expect. Once again when they walked under the street lamp it went out. They did not wait for the cold cloud again but headed in the opposite direction.

Ryan does not claim to be a psychic but he did get some kind of mental impression from this strange encounter. He felt that whatever the cloud was, it was not just a mindless meteorological phenomena. He felt intelligence in it, and malice. He still does not know what it was, but he does not want to encounter it again.

Jory (Private residence on Perry Road, Spokane, Washington)

"Katherine" and her two year old son moved into an old rental home on Perry Road in Spokane a few years ago. It was an older house with other old houses on either side of it. Shortly after Katherine moved in she noticed that small household items would disappear and then reappear later in strange places. It was odd but after all, they had just moved in and things could have been moved around as she was unpacking.

After everything was unpacked Katherine noticed that her son began talking to an imaginary friend. Once again, this was odd but when children move from one place to a new one they sometimes make up friends, until they find new ones. This imaginary friend did not go away. Katherine's friend Jamie brought her own two year old boy over. After a few visits Jamie's son began talking to the invisible friend. One evening when she and her son were over for a visit Katherine's son suddenly said, "Jory!"

He pointed to a space in the middle of the living room. No one was there. He walked over to the front door and opened it. He waited a few seconds and closed the door and said, "Bye Jory!" Katherine asked her son where Jory had gone. He pointed out a nearby window, indicating outside.

Earlier that day Katherine had noticed that her garage door was open. The garage was very old and the door was stiff. It was hard to close and even harder to get open. She and Jamie went out and after several minutes managed to close it. They returned to the house and after a few minutes they noticed that the door was open again. They went out and closed it again. Again, after a few minutes they found the garage door open. This ritual was repeated several times that day. Neither Katherine nor Jamie had wanted to admit that anything was wrong. Katherine talked with the neighbor who lived on the other side of her garage and found that they too had suffered from strange happenings.

Her neighbor would often hear the sound of a baby or child crying at night. Katherine began putting the pieces together. Her son would sometimes talk to Jory, or call his imaginary friend a baby. Katherine began experiencing childlike, poltergeist phenomenon. Houseplants were moved from their places and put in the middle of the living room. Lights would be turned on or off. Jory seemed to be very interested in the Monopoly game. Several times when she was cleaning the house Katherine would find the toy car on the floor. She would pick it up and put it away, only to find it on the floor a few minutes later.

Like all children, Jory would obey adults when they put their foot down. When her lighter disappeared, Katherine demanded that Jory return it. Shortly after Katherine made her demand, the lighter was gently placed on her lap. Jory also seemed able to affect watches. When people came into the house, their watches would usually stop working. When they left, the watches would begin working again.

In addition to the ability to move or affect objects, Jory could be seen, which is unusual for a poltergeist. One of Katherine's friends, Beth saw the apparition of a beautiful little girl. She had blue eyes, pale white skin and strangely enough, she was hairless. Another friend saw the apparition of a boy with dark brown hair. Which one was Jory? Did both visitors see what they were expecting, or were there two ghosts in the house? Then there were the two visitor who on separate occasions saw a ghost fire burning outside the living room window.

After about six months Katherine could not live with her other guests. She found another house to rent, but Jory did not want her to leave. Katherine's friend Jamie came to help her pack. They put Jamie's son and two other children to bed with Katherine's son and went downstairs to finish packing. After a few minutes they heard the children yelling upstairs. One child had a bite mark on top of his head. He told the adults that Jory had bitten him. They all went down to the living room. Jamie began reading passages from the Bible aloud. They heard the sound of a baby crying from the second floor. Eventually Jamie was yelling to keep up with the volume of the crying. Jamie and Katherine had had enough and prepared to leave. As they gathered their things they heard crashes and bangs as things were thrown against the walls on the second floor.

Katherine came back long enough to finish packing her things before moving out. Over the years she talked with other tenants and neighbors. The six months that she had spent in the house was the longest any tenant had stayed. The ghosts of children also haunted the houses on either side of hers. These houses dated to the early 1900s. Did the children live in all or one of these houses? Or was there an earlier house on the same site that burned down, leaving only the spirits of two lost children?

Off with his head (a private residence at W603 and 14th, Spokane, Washington)

Many of us are fascinated (and sometimes repelled) by mannequins. Some of them are too real for some peoples comfort level. One offshoot of this human reaction is the living mannequin. These are people will stand in stores displays and "freeze" and then change their position periodically. The world record for freezing is held by a man who was stabbed in the back by someone who wanted to prove that the mannequin was not really alive. What happens when a real mannequin or ventriloquists dummy moves without human aid? Many people will stare at store mannequins for hours, after swearing this happened, waiting for it to move again.

Something like this happened to Scott Spence of Spokane, shortly after he moved into his new house. Scott bought his house before he was married but did not like living alone. Instead of getting a cat or dog, he found a mannequin to keep him company. He named it Marcel and dressed it in an Army uniform. He finished Marcel's wardrobe by adding a woman's wig and putting a pipe in its mouth. Marcel was then placed in the living room for guests to admire.

One evening Spence was working upstairs. He heard the sound of a heavy object being dragged across the floor in the living room downstairs. The sound was like that which a high pitched squeaky wheel would make. Spence ran downstairs to investigate the noise. There was no one there.

At first he did not notice anything out of the ordinary until. he looked at Marcel. The mannequin was standing it its usual place, dressed in its uniform. This time it's head was removed from the body and resting in its outstretched hands. Unlike most ghost-hosters, who claim they kept calm, Spence admitted that he screamed in surprise and fear. When he moved in Spence saw a bat hanging from an attic shutter. He took it as an omen. Unfortunately the meaning of most omens are not clear until it is too late.

Patsy Clark's Mansion and restaurant (2208 W 2nd Ave, Spokane, WA)

In the 1890s local mining baron Patsy Clark built his dream mansion near the street named after him in West Seattle. After passing through the hands of several owners the building eventually came into the hands of a group that turned it into a restaurant in 1982. The building conversion was not an easy one. The Browne's Addition Neighborhood Association was against this change. They were not in favor of the various construction vehicles that took up parking spaces in the neighborhood. Like the cement mixers who came to pour a new floor for the basement. The neighbors would have been more upset at what was found before the basement was poured.

A few days before the concrete was poured two workmen were smoothing the dirt floor in the basement to prepare for the concrete. They discovered some unexpected artifacts amid the dirt and rocks on the floor. They found a pair of women's button-up leather shoes. The kind used in the 19th and early 20th century. They also found a few suspicious bones. They brought the shoes and bones to the restaurant manager. He was afraid of any scandals or delays in opening his business and ordered the workmen to get rid of everything. He should have held onto them.

As soon as the restaurant opened strange things began to happen. Rose Rhoades, who worked at Patsy's from its opening until 1991 saw water dripping from the ceiling onto the floor in the bar. She got a bucket and placed it on the floor to catch the water. She and a co-worker went upstairs to find out what had caused the leak. They looked everywhere but could not find a leak or standing water.

By the time they returned, several inches of water had accumulated in the bucket. She looked up and saw that the ceiling plaster had already begun to pucker and stain. She called the restaurant manager. The manager hurried past her and went into the bar to look at the leak. A few minutes later he came out of the bar yelling about the leak being a practical joke. Rhoades and her co-worker went back into the bar and looked at the ceiling. It was dry as a bone, with no water damage or staining. All Rhoades could do was look at the manager in shock. A later examination of the ceiling space above the bar showed that there were no pipes running anywhere near the spot where the leak had appeared.

In the early 1990s Tracy Hunter was a server at the restaurant. She remembered the one evening when she was setting up the empty second floor dining room. She was nearly finished when she noticed that all of the candles she had lit had gone out. She lit them all again, only to find a few minutes later that they had all gone out again. The hauntings continued.

In 1997 Debbie Martinez was working on hot August day. Martinez was on the second floor, near the restrooms doing the restaurant bookkeeping. After working quietly for several minutes she felt and eerie presence. She looked up from her books and turned around. She saw a woman in a white peignoir standing at the head of the stairs, with her hand on the railing. Martinez made eye contact with the woman, who looked at her with interest. Martinez noticed that the woman was transparent. The apparition turned away from Martinez and began walking up the stairs to the third floor…and then vanished.

In October of 1998 Doug Clark of the *Spokesman-Review* and a small party of watchers held a vigil in the restaurant. Included were the general manager, creative consultant, ex-employees, a photographer and Cindy Gardner, a Spokane psychic. The vigil had a potentially promising beginning. While they were waiting for the restaurant to close, a waiter lit a fire in the bar's fireplace. Within minutes smoke filled the room, blocked by a closed flue. According to the general manager, Jeff Sparks, he had checked the flue that morning and it had been working fine.

Once the restaurant was closed, the group of hopeful ghost watchers walked around the building. By 2 a.m. they reached the third floor. Upon entering one unlit room psychic Cindy Gardner stopped and informed the others that she sensed a negative energy and tried to dispel it. They continued touring the third floor until they came to the Bride's Room, where Gardner stopped again.

Gardner had commented that she had felt a spirit following them on the third floor. She felt that the ghost was that of a young woman. When asked about the spirit, Gardner replied that the spirit was aware of them and was proud of the house. This was an eerie experience for all of the watchers. Despite the information from the psychic, no one saw or felt anything else out of the ordinary for the rest of the night.

The real story might still be lying buried under several inches of concrete in the basement. Were the shoes cast off, along with animal bones, or was someone buried in the basement years ago? We'll probably never know, one of the ingredients of cement is lime, which has a tendency to dissolve many things, like bones.

Works Consulted

Books

Brown, Joseph C. (editor)

1974 Valley of the Strong, Stories of Yakima and Central Washington History. A Kit Publication, Yakima, WA.

Periodicals

Bogan, Christopher

26 October 1980 "Ghosts". The *Spokesman Review*, pp. D1, Spokane, WA.

Clark, Doug

1 June 1989 "When your hall is haunted, who ya' gonna call?" *Spokesman Review*, Spokane, WA.

21 October 1990 "Ghosts lurk behind walls and cellar doors". *Spokesman Review*, pp. B1 Spokane, WA.

30 October 1990 "The spooks are special in Spokane". *Spokesman Review*, pp. B1 Spokane, WA.

31 October 1991 "Ghost stories required reading for cocky trick-or-treaters". *Spokesman Review*, Spokane, WA.

27 April 1997 "Bonded, licensed psychic friend can lift city curse". *Spokesman Review*, Spokane, pp. B1 WA.

27 October 1998 "Are Patsy's ghosts real or just cooked up?", Spokesman Review, Spokane, WA, p.A1.

Creighton, Jocelyn

31 October 1994 "County has share of spooky places". Daily Record, Ellensburg, WA pp. A1.

Knutson, Kathleen

30 October 1990 "When the Spirits Move Them. "*Tri-City Herald*, Pasco, Kennewick, Richland, WA, Desert Living section pp. 1.

O'Neal, Dori

31 October 1993 "Tales from the crypt." "*Tri-City Herald*, Pasco, Kennewick, Richland, WA, pp. C1.

Internet resources

Anonymous,

1999 "The Perry House", www.crown.net/X/Stories.

Huston, Ryan

1998 "Light on the Corner", International Ghost Hunter Society: *http://www.aone.com.*

The Columbia River Gorge

Stonehenge State Park (in the vicinity of mile marker 102 on Washington State Highway 14)

What makes a place sacred or a spiritual center? Are some sacred places naturally high in supernatural energy that can be detected by sensitive people who travel there? Or can we go to any place and worship, and the power of our own belief then makes the place sacred. Or are both theories true? This question may be answered at the Stonehenge monument built by Sam Hill from the 1910s to 1930.

During the height of World War I, Sam Hill, the legendary force in the development of the Columbia River gorge was vacationing in England. One day he was a guest of Lord Kitchener, the senior British general in command of British soldiers during the war. They visited the real Stonehenge monument on the Salisbury Plain, in England. At that time archaeologists believed that the Druids constructed the entire structure around 2000 BC and performed human sacrifices there. This interpretation has now changed but Hill and his contemporaries believed it.

While they were walking among the fallen and standing stones, Hill, who was a Quaker, was struck by the folly of man. In the 4000 years since Stonehenge was built young men were still being sacrificed on the altar of war and oppression. When he returned to the United States, Hill decided to build a replica as a monument to the tragedy of World War I and in particular to remember the men from Klickitat County who died there. He wanted to construct the monument as an exact replica of what the real Stonehenge might have looked like when it was first built.

At the real Stonehenge, when the sun rises in the morning during the summer solstice on June 21st, it always shines first on a large rock east of the stone circle called the Hele stone. Hill had Astronomer W. W. Campbell of the Lick Observatory calculate the position of the Hele stone for the replica on the 8th of June 1918. The monument was dedicated a few weeks later, on the 4th of July. At that time three soldiers from Klickitat County had already died in the war. It took Hill another 12 years to complete his Stonehenge monument. It was dedicated on Memorial Day in 1930 and had a total of 12 names inscribed on the large stones. Perhaps as a final tribute to his convictions, Sam Hill was cremated after his death and his ashes were placed in a granite obelisk located on the hillside below Stonehenge.

I have been to Stonehenge several times over the last decade. It is now a state park and open during daylight hours. Exceptions to this rule are during the Vernal and Autumnal Equinoxes in March, and September when the hours of daylight and nighttime are equal and the 21st of June, the Summer Solstice, which is the longest day of the year. At these times, depending on the weather in the gorge there may be hundreds or even thousands of people there before sunrise to celebrate ancient festivals; sometimes with new twists.

In the late 1980s, I visited Stonehenge to watch the sunrise of the Summer Solstice. I had taken an astronomy course and wanted to see if the circle actually functioned as an astronomical calendar; and watch the sun rise above the Hele stone. While I was waiting for sunrise, I watched several groups of people arrive. One man had walked several miles over night to be there for the sunrise. He set out four large candles at various points within the stone circle. I had my compass with me and politely pointed out that his candles did not mark the four cardinal points of the compass. Less politely he told me to mind my own business; he instinctively knew where the compass points were.

After that, a carload of young women arrived. They had driven all night from Seattle. They wandered around the monument for several minutes, singing songs like, "*Here comes the sun...*". They passed around a bottle of red wine and ritually ate part of a loaf of whole-wheat bread and salt. One of them buried an offering at the base of the Hele stone. Another group of worshippers arrived. This group consisted of around 10 men and women dressed in gold and silver lame' robes. They stood off to the side of the monument and performed a ceremony with chanting, waving wooden rods and brandishing a dagger.

While this these activities were being performed, the sun rose. At the real Stonehenge, an observer standing between two upright stones at the foot of the altar stone will see the sun rise over the Hele stone. In the replica Stonehenge, I stood in the appropriate place but was not rewarded with the same sight. The sun rose several degrees south east of the Hele stone. According to one legend, the Hele stone was purposely placed out of alignment to stop it from being used for pagan rituals. According to another theory, the Hele stone is placed in the correct position but since the monument is located at the foot of the Klickitat Hills, the hills actually hide the suns first rays from the monument and appears from over the hills when it has moved out of position.

In the 1990s the number of people visiting the monument has grown. Will their activities convert this site into a psychic shrine? Only time will tell.

Grants Pass, OR

This story does not involve any ghosts or strange

creatures in Grants Pass but it does relate to a very special auction. On November 8th and 9th of 1997 Fain and Co. of Grants Pass held an auction of objects that they had collected over a seven-year period. One item in particular stood out in the auction list, a vampire killing kit dating to the late 19th Century.

This particular item was marketed by a Professor Ernst Blomberg. It included several things, such as an instruction manual on how to kill vampires. Among the tools included in the wooden box was a gun shaped like a crucifix, which shot silver bullets (4 included). There was a bullet mold to make more bullets and a small flask of gunpowder. Other items consisted of a wooden stake and a bottle of anti-vampire serum. This last item was empty. Hopefully it worked.

Prior to the auction, the Fain's advertised the auction list on the Internet. They recorded 50,000 hits on the vampire kit. I was unable to find out to whom the kit was sold. Let's hope it fell into the right hands.

Troutdale, Oregon

The Edgefield Poorhouse (2126 SW Halsey, Troutdale, Oregon)

Many people today have heard the expression; "You're going to end up in the poor house". We all know that this means we're in danger of some kind of financial ruin. For some reason the collective American memory has forgotten what the institutions known as poor houses really were.

In the days before the modern social welfare programs of the United States, poorhouses were established as a place where the aged, infirm, disabled, ignorant or generally indigent were placed when they could not support themselves and no family or friends could be found to take care of them. The poor house was a complex buildings and farmland located outside of larger towns, built on land donated by private individuals or municipal governments. Sometimes larger cities would have their own poorhouse. In rural areas, a poorhouse would be used jointly by all towns and villages within a county.

In some cases the poorhouses were supported by donations and taxes paid by local charities and businesses. In other cases the land was fertile or had resources that could be exploited and make enough money to keep the poorhouse running. This could be done by the...inmates...of the establishment or hired labor. I say inmates because many people placed in poorhouses were put there involuntarily and never left. With good management, many poorhouses became prosperous. Oftentimes the poorhouses were mismanaged and the inmates treated worse than animals. Whether the poorhouse was pleasant or not, the social stigma of having lived there was something that no one in the 19th or early 20th century wanted known.

Fortunately for Portland Oregon's collective historical conscience, the Edgefield was one of the most prosperous and humanely run facilities to serve as a poor house. The Edgefield Poorhouse was built in 1911 as the Multnomah County Poorhouse. A large building was built on the 330 acre site as combination dinging facility, administration offices and rooms for residents. By 1914 its fields not only fed its inmates, but the excess was sold to make over $2,000 in profits. The facility stayed open until 1947, changing from poorhouse to nursing home to suit the needs of its aging inmates.

In 1947 new social welfare programs were instituted and

the name of the poor farm was changed to the Multnomah County Home and Farm. In 1964 the tuberculosis hospital was turned into a facility for troubled children and renamed the Edgefield Lodge. In addition to the new children's treatment facility, it was still used as an elderly peoples home until it closed in 1982. The building sat vacant for several years. In 1988 the McMenamins brothers toured the decrepit poorhouse buildings offered for sale. In 1990 they were able to secure a loan that allowed them to purchase the buildings and over a period of several years restore many of them to their present condition. This includes the present Edgefield winery and brewery facilities and bed and breakfast. Over the years many employees and guests have noticed strange things happening in most of the buildings at Edgefield.

The Power Station

Before Edgefield was opened as a bed and breakfast, the power station building was opened up as a restaurant. The restaurant and restoration workers stayed in the winery wing of the poorhouse building, because it was the only portion still usable as quarters. A sheet of fabric was used to seal it off from the rest of the building. During the winter and in the middle of windstorms it would blow cold air from the vacant portion to the inhabited portions of the building. More than one employee quit or stayed away from that area due to its gothic atmosphere.

Liz and her fiancée were two of the early workers who stayed there in the early 1990s. Liz usually worked the night shift, cleaning the Power Station building and preparing it for the next days business. She would frequently stop vacuuming around 4 AM because she could feel someone standing behind her. When she turned around there was no one there. The meat grinder would turn itself on when no one was there. Sometimes the presence was so overwhelming that she would ask it to leave her alone. She was surprised that this request was usually honored and she would pass the rest of the night in peace. Usually.

One night Liz was walking between the bar and kitchen space. She was frightened when several wine glasses in the wooden rack overhead shattered, covering her with broken glass. She was unhurt but shaken up. There was not explanation for this; she was not carrying anything to hit the glasses with. She noticed that the broken glasses came from the middle of the hanging row. The glasses on the edge of the rack were undamaged.

The Black Rabbit

When the Black Rabbit first opened up, one of the cooks watched an orange roll across the floor of the kitchen. The kitchen is long and very level so gravity could not be blamed. No one saw who or what had put the orange on the floor and started it rolling. Another employee was taking some refuse down into the basement one evening. He was surprised when he came face to face with an old man. He stepped back and the man vanished.

Ryan worked for several months at the Black Rabbit as Edgefield security. One night he noticed that several pieces of silverware, particularly knives began falling off the counter. He was amazed when one knife flew through the air and buried itself in the plaster wall, across the kitchen. They removed it after several people examined it. The next morning, between the time when the cleaning staff left the building and the morning crew arrived, someone had taken several knives and stuck several of them in a row in the middle of the Power Station floor.

One of the workers had been talking with some of the old time residents during the grand opening of the Power Station. He had been amazed at various types of people who had eventually ended their days at the Edgefield. One of them had been a former circus performer. A woman who had been an expert knife thrower before her hands had begun shaking. Had she been saying hello to some old friends or making her presence known?

On a different occasion Ryan was working late night security. He was sitting in an open office when he saw a figure riding a bicycle whiz the outside window. He hurried outside and saw an old man riding along the road in front of the winery building. He hurried after the man. Just as he was close enough to stop the man, a car drove up from the side and blinded him with its headlights. When he could see again, the old man and bicycle were gone. There was no where they could have hidden.

The Winery Building

The **Althea Room** is located on the top floor of the Poorhouse Administrator's Building. It is one of the more expensive rooms, taking up the entire top floor of the building. In 1994 a family checked out in the middle of the night. They reported that in the middle of the night someone rubbing their feet awakened them. When the people have awakened they have seen the ghost of a girl or young woman standing at the foot of their bed or in the corner. Other guests have told Edgefield staff the same story. Groundskeepers and staff have seen a face looking out of the third story windows at them. This has happened on days when there have not been any guests staying in the building. When the staff members have rushed into the building and up the stairs, they found the Althea room locked and empty.

When I visited the Edgefield in 1999, the manager, Crystal called one of the tour guides, Allyse, to tell me the history of the complex and some of the ghost stories. We sat in a quiet nook in the bar for quite some time, talking. Allyse struck me as being levelheaded. She had not seen anything strange herself and was skeptical but believed in the possibility of ghosts. After talking about the various haunted rooms at the Edgefield we went to the front desk and got keys to most of the haunted rooms. It was at the Althea room that we both had a strange experience.

When we were walking to the Administrator's Building she was telling me that the ghost of a young girl. As we began climbing the steep stairs to the third floor she told me that several people had heard the voice of a girl calling out nursery rhymes at night. She started chanting,

"One two, buckle my shoe...won't you play with me?"

This was not said in her normal voice and I looked hard at her. Her expression was normal, so I guessed that she was just imitating the ghost of the little girl. We finally reached the top of the stairs and opened the door.

"So, what about the little girl?" I asked her and finished the nursery rhyme for her. She froze and looked shocked.

"Where did you hear that?" She demanded.

"You just recited the rhyme to me", I replied. She could not believe it. Allyse thought that she had been thinking to herself and not speaking out loud. She became even more excited as she looked around the room. She walked around the room looking at the furnishings and little alcove closets while I took pictures. She was convinced that there was a presence there in the attic room. Given her behavior I am inclined to believe that there was something strange going on.

Guests staying in **Room 20** may find it hard to sleep. Some guests have reported that the bed will slide away from the wall in the middle of the night.

Room 34 has a resident ghost that likes to shake people by the ankles. When they wake up, some of them have seen a tall woman standing at the foot of their beds. When they confront her, the woman disappears. She also takes vindictive action at people who offend her. In 1993 a couple and their 3-year-old daughter were staying in Room 34. The parents could not get to sleep until late because their daugher kept them up by chatting with an invisible friend.

The mother finally sat up in bed and yelled at her daughter to ignore the imaginary friend and get to sleep. The next morning when they woke up they found that someone had opened up the woman's travel bag, emptied a box of feminine hygiene products and shredded all of them. The little girl insisted that the other woman had been mad at her mother. It could have been the daughter of course, but acts of revenge like that are more characteristic of a grown woman rather than a child.

Shortly after this incident Liz Robbins, who is now the manager at the Kennedy School was inspecting this room. She had been making fun of the ghost, daring it to do something outrageous. Before she left, Liz had opened a widow and placed a heavy fan in the window. She then closed the window on the fan and left. A few seconds after she closed the door to the room, Liz heard a loud crash. She hurried back into the room and saw that the fan was no longer in the window. Somehow the window been thrown from the window sill. It had to have been thrown, because it was located several feet away from the building. It had also been unplugged, otherwise it should have been dangling from the wall outlet and, the window sash was now open all the way as if someone had thrown the window completely open in a rage.

Room 37 has it's own permanent guest. One night a couple woke up to find a woman pacing about in their room. At first they thought that she had somehow walked into their room and was disoriented or lost. They noticed that she was not dressed right. She was wearing a cloth coat and hat similar in style to those worn in the 1950s. They got out of bed and approached her to see if they could help her. She vanished. Perhaps she was looking for the equally strange man across the hallway in Room 38.

Another couple were staying in **Room 38** one night when they were awakened when their room lights came on. They saw a strange man in the room. He did not seem to notice them. He paced around the room for several seconds and then sat on the foot of their bed. The bed shifted under his weight. They watched in shocked silence as the strange man got up, walked to the door and seemed to grab a set of invisible keys from an equally invisible hook on the door, unlock it and walk out, closing the door behind him.

Bagpipers protect Room 215

Room 215 is located in the main Edgefield building. It is the second most haunted room in the entire building complex and certainly the most talked about. The building was vacant for several years between the time it was closed down and the time when the McMemanins purchased it. During that time many of the buildings suffered from neglect and vandalism. Many of the rooms and walls were covered with graffiti. Room 215 seemed to have been a favorite of a group of devil worshippers who painted a pentagram on the floor.

Before the building was opened to the public the staff tried their best to exorcise any evil influences. They removed the painted design and then painted over the floor. A group of bagpipers who were playing at the Edgefield were persuaded to play the song A*mazing Grace* as they marched around the room and hallway. This event was portrayed by one of the artists at the Edgefield in a painting on the room's door. The sound of bagpipes has been thought to exorcise evil spirits and it may have worked in part on Room 215; at least for the evil spirits, but not all.

A friendly black dog periodically awakens guests in an unusual way, by sticking its cold nose in their faces. Many guests have called the front desk complaining about the strange dog that has snuck into their room. One guest got out of bed and held off the friendly black dog that had been jumping on him and trapped the dog in the room. He called for the management and brought them to the room to remove the dog. When they opened the locked door, the room was empty. The staff have had their own share of strange events in this room too.

The staff at the Edgefield takes their job seriously. Every morning the cleaning staff changes the bedding and linen, vacuums the carpeting, cleans the windows and lays out bathrobes on the beds. Before the room is rented to a customer, a different hotel housekeeping manger goes through all of the rooms to maker sure that the cleaning staff has done their work. Late one morning, two staff members unlocked the door to Room 215 and entered. They found the doors of the linen cupboard wide open and several pieces of linen on the carpet in front of the cabinet.

They tisked tisked to themselves for a few minutes, replaced the linens and closed the doors to the cabinet. They turned to go and opened the door. There was a loud banging sound followed by a muffled thump. They turned around and saw that the linen cabinet doors were wide open again and the linen was spread across the floor, as if someone had swept it out of the cabinet onto the floor. Strange events till happen in this room.

Early in 1999 a husband and wife were staying in Room 215. They arrived in the late afternoon and retired without taking one of the interpretive tours that the Edgefield puts on several times a day. That evening, the husband was brushing his wife's hair and began humming and then began singing the song *Amazing Grace*. Both of them thought that this was very strange. The husband could not explain the strange urge he gave into. The next day they took a tour of the winery and buildings and were surprised when the tour stopped by the door of their room and explained the strange circumstances of the pentagram and later pipers cleansing it. Was this a case of a subliminal message the husband received when they checked in or the music still echoing through the room?

Some of the paranormal activity spills over into the hallway, unless there are even more ghosts. One evening two guests, a man and woman were standing in the second floor hallway. The same corridor as Room 215. They noticed an old man shambling down the hallway carrying some towels on his arm. The couple looked at each other and the man decided to follow the little old man down the hall to see what he was up to. The younger man followed the shambling older figure into the men's room. When the young man entered he found it empty. The old man has been seen quite often walking down the hallway. He is usually seen walking a small black dog.

Some guests on the second floor have been awakened by the sound of someone walking and making noise in the hallway. Several have opened their doors to investigate the noise and yell at the culprits. When they opened their doors the noises usually stop. A few people have been very surprised to find an old man and black dog standing outside the door, as if they were expecting the guest to open it. The guests usually slam the door shut in surprise. Some have reopened the door only to find the hallway empty. In addition to the little old man a woman is sometimes seen walking the phantom dog. She is described as being elderly, with tall, crazy white hair. She is always wearing a blue moo-moo type dress.

In the Mid-1990s Annie, one of the hotel employees was not feeling well. She was very pregnant and needed to lie down. She was given the keys to **Room 32**. She laid down in the bed and tried to get to sleep. Each time she began to nod-off the bed would shake violently, waking her up. After two or three episodes like this she eventually fell asleep.

Many guests at the Edgefield in the Rooms I mentioned previously and other rooms have reported having their feet or ankles grabbed or rubbed. This confused me because I could not think of anything other than a ghost with a foot fetish. After some discussion with other people I found out that in hospitals, particularly geriatric centers, touching people's feet is a common method of waking people up or checking nerve responses. It is a lot safer than shaking them by the shoulder. Could this be a remnant of the time when the Edgefield was not only a poor house, but also a health care facility?

The WineTasting Rooms

In the days before McMenamins the brewery had been used as a butcher shop. One of the butchers seems to have stayed behind. Several employees have seen a man walking around in the back of the brewery. He is dressed in an old fashioned butcher's apron and is usually seen some distance from the employees. When he is approached, he usually walks away and when he is out of sight, he seems to disappear, e. Even when he walks into a storage closet with only one entrance.

Kevin has worked in the winery for several years. He has not had too many experiences that were paranormal or strange, except for this one. One night he and a few other employees were stacking several oak casks of wine on the wooden frames. These frames are in the wine tasting room and hold several casks. They finished one stack of casks, which took hand dollies and went to get more. When they returned they found that one of the casks had been turned and was nearly falling off the rack. The casks weighed nearly one hundred pounds, there was no way short of human intervention or an earthquake that it could have been moved like that. There had not been an earthquake and none of the workers admitted to bumping or moving the cask.

Suzie has worked in the Wine Tasting Room for several years. She dispenses good conversation in large quantities and great wine in smaller portions to guests. She has had a few strange experiences in her time there. She remembers one evening, standing at the bar waiting for customers. She was alone in the building when she heard the sound of a foot skidding along the metal plate at the entrance of the Tasting Room. The only problem is that the entrance was only 15 feet away from her and no one had come in. This metal plate covers a drain gutter cut into the floor of the room. It is covered by a heavy rug. It takes a great deal of effort for someone walking over the rug and plate to make this sound. I experimented with it myself. I do not see how that noise could just happen on it's own.

In the mid-1990s Suzie was closing up the wine tasting room. She was ready to exit the room when she noticed that she had not turned the heater in the back off. She walked to the rear of the room in near darkness and surprised a white cat. It was hard for her to tell who was more frightened, her or the cat. She ran to the phone to call the front desk to get help in removing the cat. The clerk at the front desk informed her that there were no white cats at the hotel. Suzie was not in a mood to hear that kind of argument. She began looking for the cat and found that the room was now empty. She has been on the look out for a white cat ever since and has never seen one.

One day one of the women who worked as a nurse at the Edgefield when it was a public institution came by for a visit. She informed Suzie that the wine tasting room had been used as an infirmary and several elderly people had died there. There were many evenings when that woman was a nurse, when she and other nurses would go to the infirmary for medical supplies. They thought the room was haunted, even then. They would enter, turn on the lights, gather their supplies, turn off the lights and leave as quickly as possible. Many times they would turn around and look at the infirmary and see that an invisible person had turned on the lights again.

Many employees across the large property and in all of the buildings have heard their names called out from behind. The voice usually seems to come from very close. When they turn around, they find that they are alone in a building or an open field. A few of the employees who have been carrying things or intent on a task have felt a hand placed in the middle of their backs, as if someone is directly behind them and does not want to be stepped on if the employee turns around. Again, when the person who was touched turns around, there is no one there.

The ghosts do not seem to like some people at the Edgefield. These people have a hard time with doors closing and sometimes locking them inside or outside of rooms. When the facility first opened things were much livelier, as if the spirits of the Edgefield resent the changes. Since then things have quieted down somewhat, but the spirits of Edgefield still seem to be active, if less noisy.

Works Consulted

Books

Nesbit, Sharon

1995 *A History of Multnomah County Poor Farm, McMenamins Edgefield*, published by McMenamins, Portland, Oregon.

Tuhy, John

1983 *Sam Hill the Prince of Castle Nowhere*, Timber Press, Portland, Oregon.

Eastern Oregon

Baker City, Oregon

The Geiser Grand Hotel (1996 Main St., Baker City, Oregon)

The Geiser Grand Hotel was built in 1889. It was promoted as the finest hotel between Portland and Salt Lake City. The architects who designed the hotel used Austrian crystal chandeliers and mahogany trim were used throughout the lobby and hallways. In 1994 the owners decided to re-open the hotel after a complete over-hall and renovation. It took three years to finish all of the work needed. In that time the construction workers and hotel staff noticed many strange things. Toward the end of the restoration work there were three shifts of workers, 24 hours a day, seven days a week. A dozen workers quit because they were afraid of ghosts. With the recent renovations, rooms are now decorated with period furniture and antiques.

The hotel has had over a hundred years to accumulate ghosts and a checkered past that may have contributed to some of the shades that may haunt it. The hotel of course began as a Mecca for rich travelers. White-gloved waiters handed out the daily menus, written in French to customers. The hotel had one of the first elevators in the Pacific Northwest. Over the years, with changing railroad lines and financial hard times, the hotel changed its clientele. It became a casino and brothel, a veteran's hospital and eventually a derelict building when it closed its doors in 1969.

The ghosts of many haunted houses become very active during restoration work. It may be that they do not like changes to their environment. Then again, the energy and activity of the people moving around the building may give the spirits the energy they need to manifest themselves. It may also be that new people coming into a new place may be more observant and recognize the spirits when they make themselves known.

Mike Fogelson worked many nights doing finish work to the interior designs and woodwork. He saw one female apparition at least 20 times. He could not remember a night when he did not see, hear or feel something strange going on. He may have seen the dancer from the days when the hotel was a casino. This was the ghost of a woman dressed in a red corset, wearing a peacock feather hat that was popular with flappers in the 1920s. He also saw a Blue Lady, wearing a blue 1930s style dress, hat and veil.

The hotel owner, Barbara Sidway has seen the Blue Lady several times. She seems to take it in stride, though it could become aggravating. In addition to the quiet Blue Lady, there are ghostly parties going on at all hours. One night Barbara and her husband were trying to sleep in their room on the second floor. They were kept up by the sound of a loud party on the third floor, directly over their room. The music and laughter were so loud that Sidway could feel the walls vibrating under her hand. Her husband Dwight hurried upstairs to quiet the noisy guests. He followed the noise to a third floor room. As soon as he approached the door, the noise stopped. The room was empty.

Bill Harp is a cook at the hotel. He and another employee watched a large box of glassware levitate off of a counter. It rose about four feet in the air and then fell to the floor, breaking everything in it. He never believed in ghosts until he started working there. According to the Sidways, most of the employees just live with the minor aggravations like curtains being tied in knots, lights flickering on an off and the occasional loud party. Some find it easier to accept than others do.

Pendleton, Oregon

Origin of an Urban Legend? (Eastern Oregon State Hospital, Pendleton, Oregon)

Reporter Tom Forstrom used to work summers at the Eastern Oregon State Hospital in Pendleton, Oregon. He heard the following story from a full-time employee as well as a patient. In the age of mass communication and urban legends, he is sure that this story originated in Oregon and spread out and re-told by other people in other locations.

Several years ago, Oregon State Highway 30 was the main route from Portland to Pendleton. A woman was driving the highway to Pendleton late one October night. When she was within sight of the hospital her car developed a flat tire. She was trying to change the flat tire, she accidentally lost the lug nuts. While she was trying to find the nuts with the aid of her flashlight, the batteries died. She was quite frightened because she was just outside of the hospital fence and could see a light shining through one of the windows. She felt like someone was watching her.

Just as she was about to give up hope, a figure appeared behind her. She could see that it was a man, dressed in a large wool coat, wrapped tightly around him. As he approached her, he picked up the tire iron…and the woman fainted. She awoke some time later, and found herself inside her car. The door was locked, the keys were in the ignition and she was wearing a heavy wool coat.

She looked got outside of her car and found that the spare tire had been put on, and the jack and tire iron were in the trunk. She looked at the hospital and saw that all of the lights were now turned off. She got into her car and drove into Pendleton and stopped at an all night garage. The mechanic found that the spare tire had been put on using one of the lug nuts from her other three tires. He replaced the missing lug nuts. She showed him the coat, left behind by her late night rescuer. The gas station owner had lived in Pendleton for several years. He recognized the coat as being the same style that a man named Martin Poe used to wear. He told the woman that Poe had killed his wife in a murderous rage and been sent to the hospital, where he died after years of guilt. His dying wish had been to help other people to atone for his sins.

The Umatilla County library, (Pendleton, Oregon)

There are many two different versions of how Ruth Cochran's ghost came to haunt the Umatilla County Library, in Pendleton. The first explanation is that she committed suicide. Some methods of committing suicide although not pleasant are at least painless. There are also painful ways to end ones life. Eating caustic chemicals like drain cleaner is one of the most painful ways I can think of. According to some versions of Ruth's story that is what she did. Ruth was despondent over a failed love affair and decided it was better to die than continue living. One day she went down into the basement of the library and swallowed a box of lye. She was found later and rushed to the hospital, but it was too late. Ruth died, but her spirit could not rest.

Pendleton resident Harvey Thompson researched the story of Ruth Cochran's death. According to the *Pendleton East Oregonian*, Ruth was closing the library late one October night in 1947 when she suffered a cerebral hemorrhage. She decided to rest in the basement and became too weak to get out or call for help. The next morning she was found, still conscious and taken to the hospital where she died. Since that time strange things have happened in the Library.

Librarians working late at night have heard footsteps echoing between the stacks of books. Sometimes the books are knocked off the shelves when no one is there. Ruth apparently likes a little breeze in the library, because windows will open by themselves and the building lights will flicker on an off of their own accord. A library maintenance man was painting the walls in the children's room when the intercom system began buzzing repeatedly. According to the stories, Ruth tried to call for help on the intercom when she collapsed in the basement. Although some people have felt strange or even apprehensive in the library building, no one has felt threatened.

The library itself moved to a new location in 1996,

leaving the beautiful 1910s era building to be converted into a city art center. People still hear strange noises in the basement and attics but the center's director attributes those sounds to expanding pipes or animals in the attic. It may well be. It may also be that without the stacks of books Ruth had no reason to remain.

Seneca, Oregon

The Gentleman of the Grand Hotel (Seneca, Oregon)

South of John Day, Oregon is the town of Seneca. Like many of the towns and cities of Eastern Oregon, Seneca had its heyday during the mining boom of the late 1800s. Once again, like many of these boom towns, Seneca had a "Grand" hotel. The Grand Hotel in Seneca has been gone for many years, but memories of it and it's ghost have been passed down in family lore. Carla's Great Grandparents owned the Grand, decades ago. Her mother stayed there when she was a child. Carla's mother, let's call her June remembered these childhood vacations.

Most children enjoy the thrill of staying in creaky old buildings that have an air of being haunted. The Grand Hotel was too scary for June to enjoy it. She felt uneasy the first time that she entered the hotel. June was given her own room on the second floor of the hotel. The first night she stayed there she could not sleep. She laid awake for what seemed like hours.

Around midnight June heard the sound of footsteps on the balcony that circled the second story of the old hotel. She sat up in her bed and looked out of the window to see who was making the noise. She saw the figure of a man, wearing an old suit and wide brimmed hat, swinging a cane; walking along the balcony past her window. June was too frightened to get out of bed. She pulled the covers up over her head and hid in bed until morning. The hotel is gone now, but June still visits the area and whenever she passes the site where the hotel stood, she gets the shivers.

Works Consulted

Periodicals

Eberhart, George

October 1997 "Phantoms among the folios: A guide to haunted libraries", *American Libraries*, Chicago, v28, issue 9, p. 68.

Forstrom, Tom

11 October 1993 "An Oregon ghost story," Stateman Journal, Salem, Oregon, p. 1B.

Unknown

"Restored hotel has ghostly legends", *LaGrande Observer*, LaGrande, Oregon, p.1.

Internet sources

Monroe, Carla

1998 Hotel Haunting, *www.rpi.net.au/~ghostgum/castle.html.*

The Northwest Coast

ASTORIA

Ft Stevens State Park, Astoria, Oregon

The primary tourist attractions at Ft Stevens State Park are the empty concrete bunkers that once housed the two big guns at Battery Russell. Tourists are unaware of the fact that there are several other gun emplacements nearby that are not part of the state park, or that the original gun emplacements at Ft Stevens date to the Civil War. Or that the gun emplacements are haunted.

During the War of 1812 British warships blockaded the mouth of the Columbia River and cut off supplies to Fort Astoria. This was a lesson United States politicians and military planners did not forget. In 1840 they discussed plans to establish United States Army forts at the mouth of the Columbia River, but nothing was done until the 1860s. The Civil War motivated the War Department to look to the security of the Union in the Pacific. Confederate cruisers had attacked Union shipping in the Pacific. They may have been sheltering at the British naval base in nearby Victoria, Canada. There were also concerns over the growth of the Army of Maximillian of Mexico. With these potential threats, the Army ordered the construction of two forts to guard the mouth of the Columbia River.

In the summer of 1863 Captain George Elliot began work that took nearly two years to finish. He constructed roads, earthworks and emplacements for over 40 guns at Fort Stevens. Only 29 cannons were mounted in January of 1865. The guns, some of which were cast in the War of 1812, remained in place until the turn of the century, when the War Department ordered the construction of new guns.

There were several batteries with gun emplacements constructed at Fort Stevens Batteries Lewis, Walker, Pratt,

Freeman, Smur, Clark and Russell. The last bunker and gun emplacements to be finished were Battery Russell. The two 10 inch diameter guns of the battery were in place by 1908. The guns were designed to fire a 617 pound shell 16,290 yards or roughly 9 miles! The batteries of Fort Stevens watched the Pacific Ocean for 40 years before they were called to duty. On the 21st of June 1942 a Japanese submarine commanded by Captain Meji Tagami surfaced off the coast and fired several rounds at Fort Stevens from their deck gun. The closest hit the beach 300 yards in front of Battery Russell. This was the only instance of United States soil being attacked by a foreign enemy in the 20th Century.

In 1947 the gun emplacements were decommissioned and the guns were removed. A few years later Ft Stevens State park was commissioned. Most of the visitors at Ft Stevens are there during daylight hours, but some visitors stay to watch the sun set over the horizon. A few of them have been treated to other sights and sounds. People walking along the old road near Battery Russell have heard the sound of a metallic ringing or clanging, like a swinging chain or metal banging on metal. The sight of a flashlight, moving along the road usually accompanies this sound, as if it is lighting a path along the road. The light and sound will approach people on the road and get so close that the tourists have seen the outline of a man, holding the flashlight. At that point, the light and noise always cease and disappear. Some people think that this may be the ghost of a park night watchman or guard patrolling the road.

Bandage Man (the vicinity of Cannon Beach or Seaside, OR)

The bandage man is a creature that has passed from first hand accounts into a coastal legend with many different spins and variations in this story. It is unknown if he is a living being or a ghost. I have heard that Bandage Man is the ghost of an accident victim, perhaps a logger, who died while being driven into town. He may have been an escaped inmate from an insane asylum, living in the woods, who liked to eat dogs or sometimes just drink their blood. I have even heard that he may be a Sasquatch that somehow put on rags for clothing. I do not think that he has been described as a space alien. Yet!

Despite these mutations to the Bandage Man's origins, the story of his activities seems to be fairly straightforward. People driving into Cannon Beach from Highway 26 should be very careful when they reach the intersection of 26 with U.S. Highway 101. People driving that stretch of road at night in pick-up trucks or open top vehicles should beware. Bandage Man may jump in the back of their vehicle. He may pound on the cab of a truck, or break windows and scare the drivers then He jumps out of the vehicle or simply disappears. He usually leaves behind a bloody bandage or the smell of rotting flesh.

I have spoken with the Oregon State Police in Astoria. Their patrol territory includes Canon Beach. They have not had any calls about any strange hitchhikers near Cannon Beach for several years. In his book, Oregon's Ghosts & Monsters Mike Helm includes a long tale about Bandage Man.

PHANTOM SHIP IN THE COLUMBIA RIVER

The Daily Astorian, Jan. 28, 1881

Capt. E.D. Brock of the steamer Westport furnishes us with the particulars of some mysterious object seen on the Columbia River on Friday night last between 8 and 9 o'clock. What it was is yet a mystery to all who witnessed it, and that some light might be thrown on the subject we give this statement from Captain Brock, the truthfulness of which is vouched for by all on board.

He says, "I left Astoria for Westport via Hungry Harbor at 5 o'clock on Friday last. When I reached Pillar Rock, I saw two lights in range of Woody Island supposing them to be on shore, but as I neared Brookfield, the lights came along up the ship channel. I thought then that they were the lights of the bark *Webfoot.* I stopped at Brookfield to land freight during which time the object got as far as the Fisherton cannery. When I started again I kept after it in the ship channel and constantly gained on it.

When I reached Bay View, I was within 200 yards of the object which was then on my port bow, and near shore when I remarked to the purser who was in the pilot house that it was about time the ship (as we supposed it was) was keeping out from shore. I put my wheel to port to give her more room. I gained all the time and when at Skamokawa, we were side by side not more than 200 feet apart.

I was just about to blow the whistle when the lights disappeared and nothing more could be seen. One was a bright light which appeared to be hung on the mast head; another was a red light appearing to be on the mizzen mast, and every few moments, we could see a number of small lights as they were on deck. The object before its disappearance was moving up river against a strong northeasterly breeze." The *Webfoot* did not leave Astoria until the following Sunday morning and no other vessel was in that part of the river at the time. What it was is a conundrum and could perhaps only be solved by the author of the Flying Dutchman.

Bandon, Oregon

Bandon is a little town south of Coos Bay that hosted it's own French Chef in the early 1990s. The fact that this particular culinary expert had been dead for over a hundred years did not bother his Ghost-hoster, Georgia Lubeck. Lubeck moved to Bandon from San Carlos California. She had been attempting to learn how to channel spirits along the same lines advocated by Jane Roberts in her *Seth* books. Lubeck was surprised when she channeled the spirit of a 17th century chef named Pierre Claude Andre du Vall.

Lubeck was a mediocre cook until this strange happening. She took advantage of her spirit contact and learned to cook with his help. This all sounds very strange and stereotypically Southern Californian to be sure but it did not stop the skeptics and scoffers from buying her book, *Ghost*

Cooking, which included several recipes that went through several printings.

Newport Oregon

The Oar House Bed & Breakfast (502 SW 2nd, Newport, Oregon)

The Oar House sits on a hillside some distance from Newport's beach, but the inhabitants of this house can see the ocean clearly from the old fashioned "Widow's Walk" built on top of its third story. You can identify the Oar house by the two crossed oars nailed to its wall. If a building ever deserved to be haunted it is the Oar House. According to local legend the house was built in 1900 using boards and timbers that its owner collected on the beach after shipwrecks. The more shipwrecks, the more rooms were added. Today the house has five guest rooms.

The house was originally built as a temporary boarding house for the sailors or dock workers that visited Newport from time to time. According to it's present owner the rest of the Oar House's story is partly fact and partly legend that has been retold and embellished over the past decades.

In the late 1920s the clientele at the Oar House changed from sailors and dock workers to prostitutes and their customers. This change in business went on for many years. In the 1930s a young woman from the mid-west came to Newport to meet her fiancé, who was arriving in Newport either as a ship's passenger or a member of the crew. No one knows the young woman's name, so let's call her "Mary".

Mary needed a place to stay while she waited, so she went to the first building that looked like a boarding house to get a room. She told her story to the Landlady/Madam, who was sympathetic. Mary was given a room on the third floor. In exchange for her room, Mary worked as a maid. She did not mind the work or the clientele, because she had privacy in her little room and she could easily see the harbor from the Widow's Walk just above her. The days turned to weeks and the weeks turned to months. Mary eventually realized that her fiancé was not going to meet her. She threw herself out the window of her small apartment and died when she hit the ground far below. Despite her death, Mary has not left the Oar House.

Jan, the present owner purchased the house in 1993, despite the stories the former owner told her. One evening he was in the guest sitting room reading a newspaper. It was a quiet night because there were no guests. As time passed he began to feel as if someone was watching him. He looked up at the ceiling. An interesting feature of this room is a small glass hatch or trapdoor leading from the sitting room to the room directly above. He thought that he saw someone looking down at him from above. He quickly walked upstairs and checked but found the room was empty. After searching the house he found his wife in the laundry room. She denied spying on him and he believed her. In order to get from the upstairs room with the trap door, she would have had to pass him in the sitting room to go down into the laundry room.

On another occasion the landlord and his wife were tired and planned on taking an afternoon nap together. Their bedroom was on the third floor, Mary's old room. That no longer bothered them, since they had been living there for so many years. The landlord walked up to the bedroom and laid down in the big double bed they used. A few minutes later he heard the sound of footsteps on the stairs. Once again, there were no guests in the house, so he thought that his wife was coming to bed. He was lying on the bed, facing away from the bedroom door. He did not turn around when the door opened. He heard footsteps crossing the floor and felt the bed move as someone laid down beside him. He turned around to talk to his wife, only to find himself lying alone on the bed.

There have not been any spectacular events like this recently. Jan does not disbelieve in the existence of ghosts, but it will take a lot to convince her of their existence. There have been a few incidents that have helped her keep an open mind though. Several guests have slept in the third floor room and noticed strange things. During the summer several guests who slept in the third floor room reported waking up in the middle of the night because of the extreme heat. It was hotter in the attic than the house had been during the middle of the day and the windows were open to let the cool air inn. Was this some kind of strange, natural thermo-dynamic transfer of heat rising from the basement to attic or something less natural?

A few years ago Jan's daughter was married and several family friends were guests in the Oar House. One of her daughter's girlfriends stayed in the third floor room. She came down to breakfast after her first night there. She complained that she had not been able to sleep. They told her that she was probably just excited over the upcoming wedding. The next morning she came downstairs and told everyone that she had not slept well again. She asked Jan if the bedroom was haunted. Jan was speechless. She had not mentioned the reputation of the third floor bedroom to anyone.

Several guests have asked Jan what she thinks of the ghost. Jan replies that Mary is a friendly ghost. Mary may not show herself, but is proving by her absence that she is happy with the way that that Jan is keeping up the house. If Mary were unhappy, Jan feels she would make herself felt or heard.

The Yaquina Bay Lighthouse (Yaquina Bay State Park, Newport, Oregon)

The US Lighthouse Service constructed the Yaquina Bay lighthouse in the summer of 1871. It was lighted in November of the same year. It did not resemble the typical lighthouses we expect to see today. The lighthouse is a two-story caretaker's house with an attached, square three-story lighthouse tower. It was one of four of this style of lighthouse built in Oregon and is the second oldest lighthouse still standing in Oregon. The lighthouse was only used for three years, from 1871 to 1874.

In 1874 it was de-commissioned in favor of the Yaquina Head lighthouse, three miles north of Newport. Over the next 60 years various state and federal agencies used the lighthouse and caretaker's house. In 1934 the Oregon State highway department purchased the buildings and surrounding property for a park. The park caretaker lived in the house until 1948 when they decided to demolish the deteriorating structure. A concerned citizen's group lobbied to save the buildings. They were successful, and the lighthouse is now run by the Lincoln County Historical Society as a museum and park.

According to folklore and history there are two ghosts that inhabit the old lighthouse. The first ghost is that of a large redheaded sailor, with an emaciated, skull-like face. This apparition may be that of Evan MacClure, captain of a Yankee Whaling ship. In 1873 MacClure and his first mate Bill Brewster had a fight over a woman in Hawaii and MacClure cut off Brewster's ear. When their ship sailed again, Brewster led a mutiny and put MacClure over the side of the ship in a small boat.

In January of 1874 there was a violent storm along the Oregon coast. Some local people were standing on seaside cliffs watching the storm waters break over the Devil's Punch Bowl near the Lighthouse. They watched a small boat wash up on the rocks and a man with red hair climbed out. In the light of the storm they saw that his face was almost skeletal. Suddenly a wave washed over the rocks, taking the boat and man with it. The boat was recovered, but not the man.

That spring the local sea rescue team was launched several times to answer help calls for help. No shipwrecks were ever found. Stories of banging and clanging of chains and doors opening and closing and strange sightings were told up and down the coast. In one instance a tall, gaunt man with red hair entered a bar in Newport and ordered a beer. He disappeared when it was served to him. He appeared to a frightened farmer's wife and declared that he needed two things to find his final rest. One was a place to stay and the second was someone to share his ghostly existence. He may have found both at Yaquina Bay. According to legend, when the lighthouse was shut down in 1874, MacClure moved in. Many people had seen the light house beacon lit, even though the oil reservoirs had been emptied for weeks.

That same year, a ship landed at Newport and a man calling himself Trevenard came ashore. He surveyed the town and arranged for his daughter Zina (sometimes she is referred to as Muriel) to stay in the small hotel until he returned in a few weeks. He never returned which is another mystery. Suspecting nothing was wrong, Zina quickly mixed in with the local young people and went out on many of their social gatherings.

In December of 1874 she joined a group that had decided to investigate the deserted lighthouse. While they were looking around the lighthouse they discovered a secret wall panel and metal door in the lighthouse third floor closet. When they removed the metal door they found a tunnel or chute leading down. They left the metal door and wainscoting on the floor and prepared to leave. They were preparing to lock the door when Zina noticed that she had left her handkerchief in the lighthouse. She reentered the building to search for it. After several minutes of waiting Zina's friends walked back toward the lighthouse to find her. They heard screams for help coming from the lighthouse.

After several agonizing seconds of delay, they opened the front door. They did not find Zina. Instead they found a pool of warm blood on the floor of one of the upstairs bedrooms. A trail of blood drops led upstairs, where her handkerchief was found lying on the floor of the closet where the hidden door had been found earlier. They also found that the metal door and wainscotting had been replaced. Zina was never seen again. Rumors continued for a hundred years about strange lights and figures seen at night in the old lighthouse.

In 1982 a hitchhiker stopped and camped on the porch of the old lighthouse. He intended to go into town looking for work. In the middle of the night he was awakened by the sound of the front door opening and a yellow light coming from within the lighthouse. A woman left the building and walked to where he was lying. A large man followed her out of the house and paused on the front porch. The woman told the man that he would find work in town, which he did. She and the man went back into the house. That same evening the captain of a tugboat and small plane pilot reported seeing the lighthouse beacon on.

In the early 1990s a local volunteer group raised

$250,000 to restore the aging structure. In 1996 restoration efforts were completed, and the beacon was relit. The lighthouse is open to the public as a museum from 12-4 PM each day and it is staffed by volunteers. Walt Muse oversees activities at the lighthouse. He has spoken with many visitors about the ghostly history of the lighthouse. Many have reported eerie sensations when walking through the building. Some have walked by late at night and reported a light emanating from a second floor room. At first Muse thought this was due to overactive imaginations, until he saw it. After several minutes he believed that it could be explained by light from the beacon on the top floor shining through loose floorboards into the second floor rooms.

The people I spoke with have not seen or heard anything strange, but are ready to answer questions about the popular stories and history of the area. The secret door and tunnel are open to the public. They are much smaller than I expected. The bloodstains are now covered over by a fresh coat of paint. One thing more difficult to explain are the pictures he has received from tourists who took photographs of the lighthouse. They show some kind of filmy figures passing in front of the camera lens.

There are several stories about the Yaquina Bay lighthouse, which conflict in some details, like the name of the missing girl. I have summarized the most popular stories here. I recommend reading Helm's account ***in Oregon's Ghosts and Monsters*** *for a longer and more detailed version of the hauntings.*

Works Consulted

Periodicals

Hanft, Marshall

1964 "The Cape Forts: Guardians of the Columbia", *Oregon Historical Quarterly*, Salem, Oregon, v.65, p. 325-359.

Kessinger, Cathy

28 January 1999 "Historic lighthouse near Newport, Oregon shrouded in mystery", Seattle Post-Intelligencer, Seattle, WA, p. 5.

Moore, Shery

31 October 1993 "Tales from the crypt", Tri-City Herald, Kennewick, Washington, p. C1.

Reed, Ione

19 November 1972 "The haunted lighthouse", *Eugene Register-Guard*, Eugene, Oregon, p. 2.

Stiles, Mark

1 June 1992 "Louie's home on the mantel to stay", *Longview Daily News*, Longview, Washington p. C8.

Unknown

30 July 1990 "Bandon Woman says French ghost gives her some spirited recipes", *Statesman Journal*, Salem.

Vorpahl, Bev

18 October 1998 "You may run into a spirit when visiting Oregon lighthouses", Spokesman-Review, Spokane, WA, p.G3.

Internet sites and documents

Lighthouse illuminations of another kind, *hallowee.gstis.net.*

Strange Critters

Although this book was meant to describe the ghostly heritage of the Pacific Northwest, it would not be complete without a discussion of the supernatural and non-supernatural creatures of the region. I use the word critter as a catch-all category for the animals described in this chapter rather than monsters. Monsters are unnatural creatures whereas a these animals are a part of the natural world, whether they be godlike or natural. Some of these stories contain large, strange and exotic animals, some mythical some not. The term Critter just seems to fit. The Native Americans had several stories of strange critters living in the high mountains and lakes of the Pacific Northwest.

One critter was the *A-yah-hase,* a half snake/half deer critter with two heads, each with a pair of horns. Whether there was only one who moved quickly or a whole race of them is unknown, but there were many sightings in the mountains. There were also many stories about a little people called the *Kwak-wa-etai-mewh.* They lived in the north and sometimes traveled down into "settled" areas. Along with the little people there was also a race of water giants.

The upper Chehalis and Nisquallies told stories of the *Pissah.* The *Pissahs* were giants that lived in the water. There was a lake near Chehalis that had been inhabited by *Pissahs* The *Pissahs* used to kidnap people who went to the lake for water and make them slaves or would eat them. The Native Americans climbed up a hill overlooking the lake. They lit a large fire and heated large stones. Once the stones were red hot, they threw them down into the lake, which dried it up and destroyed the *Pissahs*. Native American guides pointed out one of the stones to Euro-American travelers in the 1850s. The Native Americans always left a salal leaf by the stone on entering the site of the lake, which was then a prairie. Was this really a remnant of a prehistoric battle between good and evil or a folk tale invented to explain a strange, rounded boulder found in a dry lake bottom?

On the Trail of Bigfoot

There was a species of hominid or great ape called *Gigantopithecus*. What we know about *Gigantopithecus* has come from fossils. Based upon this evidence, the *Gigantopithecus* was a vegetarian creature that easily stood over six feet high. Millions of years ago these great apes ranged out from southern Asia during a period when the planet was covered with vast forests. Like many of the other man-like creatures, they became extinct. Some people looking for a natural explanation for Bigfoot have speculated that the *Gigantopithecus* spread out from Asia to North America several million years ago. Where the Asian *Gigantopithecus* died out, their North American relatives survived.

The Native Americans of the Pacific Northwest had many names for the hairy people of the woods. The common modern name of Sasquatch was probably derived from the coastal Salish word; *se'qec*. There are many more names from Native Americans from The Dalles north to Alaska and south into California. There are many stories about the Sasquatch. Most agree that they were definitely not *Elip Tillicum* (or demons). They were living beings but were not human either.

Almost all legends describe them as gigantic and smelling badly. Other stories about the Sasquatch say that they resemble human beings, but they do not speak human languages.

One Klikitat story describes them in very human like terms. They were not created or born when demons ruled the earth, but were born afterward. Although they were seen in the lowlands west of the Cascades, they had dwellings beyond the mountains, where they acted like human beings. They hunted, fished and lived in communities. Some were friendly and others were thieves and very dangerous.

The Stalo Indians who lived in the Lower Frasier Valley had many stories about the *se'qec* who lived in the mountains nearby. These men of the woods were more than 8 feet tall and frequently left behind footprints 20 inches long. They had the power to put people to sleep by merely touching them. Like many other Sasquatch stories they would raid camps and houses, taking food, children and women. They had one story where a woman was captured by a *se'qec* who took her for a wife. She came back to her people with hair growing over her body, unable to speak her tribal language. It took the power of several Shamans to return her to normal. In later times some *se'qec* were seen by hunters. She asked the hunters not to shoot them, because they could be members of her family.

Another Stalo tradition came from the Port Hammond area, in British Columbia. This series of stories described two different species of *se'qec.* There was a big timber giant and a small, meaner one. The second creature, called a *siyeye* carried a magic stick. With this stick it wold hit the tree trunk three times and knock the trees down. The Lummi Indians of the Puget Sound had many sightings of these tree strikers. These *siyeye* could act as guardian spirits and lend their power to other people. Some of them could also appear and disappear at will.

David Thompson and the snow monster?

Out of this folklore and oral tradition, there are historic accounts of Bigfoot sightings recorded in the early 1800s. In 1811 David Thompson saw footprints that later readers have interpreted to be those of a Sasquatch. He was travelling through the outlands of British Columbia in the winter when he came on a set of footprints in the snow. The track was 14 inches long and 8 inches wide. He noted that the footprint had only four toes and that each toe had a claw four inches long. He also noticed that the ball of the foot was indented deep into the snow, while the heel was not well marked. This could have been the result of whatever creature it was had been standing on the forward part of it's foot.

The tobacco gambit

In 1924, a 34-year-old construction worker named Albert Ostman had a Sasquatch experience. After a busy construction season he decided to take a vacation in the Toba Inlet of British Columbia. He did not find any gold, but got more than he bargained for. After a week of camping and hiking in the woods he awoke to find that his camp had been vandalized. A few nights later he awoke to find that he had been picked up (sleeping bag and all), and was being carried through the woods by a kidnapper he could not see.

When daylight came he saw that his captor was human like, but huge and covered with long reddish fur. It took him to a location where three other creatures waited. Ostman interpreted this to be a family unit, with a mother, father and two children, both a boy and a girl. He stayed with them for a week, trying to figure out a plan of escape. He still had his rifle but did not want to shoot any of them. He began chewing tobacco and offered some to the male, who promptly ate it.

While the male Sasquatch was doubled over in pain, Ostman tried to run away. He was pursued by the female Sasquatch. She followed him for several minutes until he was able to scare her away by firing his rifle over her head. He traveled through the woods until the next day when he found a logging camp where he got help from the lumberjacks. He did not tell the story of his abduction until the 1950s, when he heard of other Bigfoot stories.

Bigfoot at Camp Bonneville (Near Vancouver, Washington)

I remember my father telling a story about something that happened to a friend of his. In the 1960s he was in the National Guard. On one of his drill weekends he and his section were at Camp Bonneville, in southwest Washington. One of the soldiers left their positions in search of a "green latrine" in the woods. The isolated spot he chose was near one of the Camp dumps. Shortly after he arrived he heard the noise of heavy bodies moving through the garbage dump. He turned around and saw four or five tall, furry creatures rooting through the piles of garbage. They turned and looked at him. There was a stand-off for several seconds until he remembered to run away. The creatures headed in the other direction. By the time the soldier gathered some friends to investigate there was no trace of a Bigfoot or any other creatures in the vicinity of the dump. Everyone was convinced it was a family of bears, but he denied that theory.

Bigfoot Research

To the more pragmatic reader, these stories and the hundreds of sightings can be explained away as a mixture of imagination, mistaken identity and outright fabrication. The truth becomes embellished, until a close-up sighting of large bear turns into a legendary battle with the reclusive Sasquatch. Researchers, scientists and just plain folks have speculated on the origin and reality of Bigfoot. Is it real, or is it the need for human beings to clarify events that they cannot explain or put down to normal events. People, all people want to explain mysterious events somehow.

The Sasquatch has often been blamed for the disappearances of children. This may have been due to foreign Indians or Europeans in Native territory. They would be dressed in strange clothes and ornaments, or would not be seen, only their footprints would be remain. Tracks observed in the snow like those seen by Thompson are not a good gauge of the original size and shape of the creature that created them. A track may be several days old before it is seen. In that time it could have melted and refrozen several times, changing the shape of the track. Then again, most trackers and explorers should be familiar with this process.

There have been efforts to formalize the study of the Sasquatch. One serious researcher is anthropologist Grover Krantz of Washington State University in Pullman. He has spent many years studying thousands of footprints, hair, bone and skin samples. He has refined the analysis methods used in examining Bigfoot evidence. He has specialized in the bio-mechanics of the Sasquatch foot. This includes better methods of making casts of foot and handprints to analyze. He has been able to identify several separate individuals that are distinct because of size, deformities or injuries. He has also made attempts at estimating height and weight based upon comparisons between Bigfoot evidence and known human like apes. He has found interesting details like finger/foot print sworls and lines in some of the higher quality casts. One of the pieces of evidence that Krantz has looked at is a piece of film taken by Roger Patterson in the 1960s.

In 1967 Roger Patterson and Bob Gimlin were looking for evidence of a bigfoot in California's Bluff Creek Drainage. They returned with a 28 foot long piece of 16mm movie film that has since been the center of controversy ever since it was exhibited. Krantz examined the film many times and in his professional opinion the figure was a genuine Bigfoot. This was based on the way the arms moved in time with it's stride. This has been disputed recently.

In December of 1998, Chris Murphy, a Bigfoot researcher and teacher at the British Columbia Institute of Technology examined a copy of the Patterson movie, frame by frame. He magnified some frames 100 times. In four of the frames he found a small, geometirc object attached to the Bigfoot's body. In his opinion, the object was either a bell or a clasp of some kind. He send a picture of this object to Cliff Crook, who runs Bigfoot research center called "Bigfoot Central" in Washington. He interpreted the object as being a fastener or zipper end for a Bigfoot suit. Later, a man living in Yakima Washington made a statement that he wore the suit for Patterson. People who believe the film is genuine have countered this.

In the 1960s the Walt Disney Studio's make-up men made statements saying that they could not have made a Bigfoot costume that looked as real as the creature in the Patterson film. Bob Gimlin was with Patterson at the time the film was made and still swears that the sighting was not a hoax. Detractors to the film pointed out that shortly after the Patterson film was made, other motion pictures like Kubrick's *2001* were made with actors dressed in very convincing costumes. The debate continues as this book goes to press. The man who claims that he wore the Bigfoot costume is represented by a lawyer. He will not speak publicly, until he finishes negotiating a movie deal for his story rights.

Despite his criticism of the Patterson film, Cliff Crook believes in the existence of Sasquatch. He came face to face with one in 1956. He investigates many of the 300-400 reports of Bigfoots that he receives every year and has high hopes that he will encounter one again.

Claude (Seen along the mouth of the Columbia River)

In 1937 the crew of the Columbia River Lightship and her tender were treated to their first sight of a sea critter they named "Claude". According to L.A. Larson, the mate of the lightship they saw a creature about 40 feet in length. A portion of it's body was taken up by a long, whip like tail. It had a long round body and a neck that was about eight feet long. He summed the whole creature as looking mean and snakey. He and the members of the crew studied the critter for several minutes with binoculars. Some members of the crew wanted to put out a boat and get close, but the officers refused to allow it.

In 1937 the Captain of the trawler *Viv* reported seeing a strange creature. It was long and sinewy, about 40 feet in length. It was about four feet in diameter at its round middle.

Unlike Larson's description, the *Viv's* Captain reported that this particular creature was covered with tan colored hair and had a head that was similar to an overgrown horse. He was seen several times over the next few years at the Columbia Bar and in the vicinity of Astoria.

Chris Anderson was the Captain of the schooner *Arpo*. He and his crew saw Claude several times. They watched the predatory critter steal 20 pound fish from their hooks. He described Claude as having a head like a camel with a bent snout. He was several feet long and covered with long gray fur. Claude was seen regularly at the mouth of the Columbia River until the 1950s when he either moved on or died. Or did he?

In 1989 Donald Riswick used to fish along the Shoo Fly drift, which is located east of the city of Astoria. He was gillnetting on his 28 foot long boat. It was a powerful boat with a 225 horse power engine. One September night he was trailing a net that was several hundred feet long and 34 feet deep. He and his assistant had let their net sit for an hour and a half when they decided it was time to pull in their catch. The water at the drift was 80 feet deep. As they pulled in the net with a motorized winch they gathered a half dozen or so fish that had been caught. They had only 500 more feet of net to pull in when the net snagged on something very large and very heavy.

They had been drifting with the current as they pulled in the net when it began to unreel. Whether it was because they had netted something stationary and the momentum of the boat was pulling against it or they hooked something that was swimming against the net, they could not tell. The bow of the boat began to sink. Riswick quickly ran to the controls and opened up the throttle of the engine. They pulled free from whatever they had hooked. He could not understand, the net was only 34 feet deep and the depth of the water was 80 feet. They could not have snagged on a piling or sunken obstacle. When they finally pulled the net out of the water they found a hole big enough to drive a mini-van through.

He told his story to several other fishermen who

suggested various theories about the strange event. Could he have snagged a sea lion, a whale or one of the few 2,000 pound sturgeon that have been spotted on the Oregon Coast? Or could Claude still be swimming along the mouth of the Columbia River?

A Spirit Snake? (Turnbull National Wildlife Refuge (Washington State)

In the 1980s the Healy family was vacationing in the Turnbull Wildlife Refuge and caught a small snake they named Slinky. The snake seemed harmless and the family's two children wanted to take the snake home with them. Instead, the father posed for a picture, holding the snake. They released the snake who slithered away. When the family returned from their trip they turned in the film to have it developed.

When they got the prints back from the photo lab there was a picture of Mr. Healy, with his hands spread, holding thin air. The picture was perfectly developed, with no flaw on it or the film. Where did the snake go? Can dead snakes become ghosts or did they pick up something else?

Works Consulted

Books

Dinsdale, Tim

1972 *Monster Hunt*. Acropolis Books, Washington.

Krantz, Grover S.

1992 *Big Footprints: A Scientific Inquiry into the Reality of Sasquatch.* Johnson Printing Company, 1180 South 57th Court, Boulder, Colorado 80301.

Strasenburgh, Gordon R. Jr.

1979 "Perceptions and Images of the Wildman", reprinted in *The Scientist Looks at Sasquatch II,* edited by Roderick Sprague and Grover S. Krantz. Anthropological Monographs of the University of Idaho No. 4. University of Idaho Press, Moscow.

Periodicals

Anonymous

January 1999 "Enthusiasts at odds over Bigfoot film", *Stars and Stripes*, p.10.

Associated Press
29 January 1999 "Lawyer says he represents man who wore Sasquatch suit in vintage footage", *Tri-City Herald*, Kennewick, WA.
Ciams, Peter
24 September 1967 "Colossal Claude and the Sea Monsters," The *Oregon*, Portland, Oregon.
Gibbs, George
1955 - 1956 "Account of Indian Mythology in Oregon and Washington Territories". *Oregon Historical Quarterly* 56 (4): 293 - 325, 57 (2)pp. 125 - 167, edited by Fila Clark.
Riswick, Donald V.
1998 "Two River Tales," *CUMTUX*, the Clatsop County Historical Society Quarterly, Vol. 18, no. 1, Astoria, Oregon
Roberts C.R.
29 November 1998 "Bigfoot film:Disproof may be in the details" The *News Tribune*, Tacoma, WA. p.B1.
Rosellini, Lynn
25 January 1999 "Not so big after all", *U.S. News & world Report*, p.61.
Wasson, David
4 February 1999 "Bigfoot Believers Say Film No Fake", *The Herald-Republic*, Yakima, WA.

Internet Resources

Walgamott, Andrew
7 December 1998Former Bothell resident says Bifgoot film shows man in a fur suit," *Northwest News*. www.nwnews.com/eitions/19981207/ local4.html.

Some thoughts on Ghost Hunting

This portion of this book is dedicated to a discussion of the science of paranormal research. To some readers it may appear that it is also dedicated to skepticism and promoting a disbelief in ghosts and the paranormal, since many of the latest advances in parapsychological research have found reasonable explanations for some hauntings. I would be doing a disservice to you the reader if I did not present some of the latest information on paranormal research. Just because a new scientific examination of a haunting exposes it as something as commonplace as infra sonic sounds or an electrical short does not mean that all hauntings are caused by the same natural phenomenon.

I know that many readers have lived or currently live in a haunted house. I think that most of them would be relieved to find a rational explanation for the strange things happening in their houses. If they can view things in a rational manner and conduct their own research even if they cannot explain the phenomenon, then they will be better prepared to deal with a true ghost.

Natural phenomenon mistaken for hauntings

One of the common occurrences people notice in hauntings is strange glowing lights. This might come from a human spirit but it can also come from various natural phenomenon. The reason people call ghostly lights ghostly, is that they are uneven. Human beings produce lighting with incandescent and fluorescent light bulbs that is regular and steady. We get used to it, and consider it to be natural. When we go out in truly natural settings, we suddenly become aware of the uneven quality of the light outside. Sometimes this shift can be confusing, if we go from artificial light suddenly into natural light with no transition, say when lights go out and a room is flooded with moonlight.

In the dark or under moonlight natural substances can glow or take on a different appearance. There are some plants that have phosphorus in them and glow at night. Mineral deposits under water can glow under moonlight, as can swarms of insects. Because we are used to artificial lighting, it can appear strange. When we take a picture of it, depending on the shutter speed of the film, the waver may appear or it may not.

Spirit photographs have been produced for over one hundred years. In some cases the photographs show transparent to solid looking shapes that were not in the frame when the picture was taken. If you have a ghost photograph please try and eliminate the non-paranormal causes. One thing that will often trip people up is a camera strap that accidentally swings up in the picture frame the second the picture is taken. The camera strap is usually out of focus and is sometimes moving so fast that it will appear to be transparent.

Another common things mistaken for ghosts are balls of light in the picture. If there is a light source like a lamp within the shot, this can bounce off a mirror or glass, creating ghost images. This happened to me when I was taking pictures of the bar in the Seven Gables Inn in Olympia. A stack of wine glasses reflected sunlight onto the mirror behind the bar, creating a series of blurry images above the glasses. This is very true in the case of some of the newer digital cameras that use flashes. I have seen dozens of digital photographs with dozens of balls of light in them. The difficult part of proving whether this kind of photograph is a trick of the light or a paranormal being is that there are no negatives to be examined by a laboratory.

Infrasound

Sound. Whether we are hearing impaired or not, we all have a concept of sound, because it's all around us, but what is sound? When you speak, your vocal cords vibrate back and forth. One vibration is called a cycle. The number of times your vocal cords cycle (or vibrate) a second is their frequency, called a Hertz. One cycle a second is one Hertz. Twenty cycles a second equals a frequency of 20 Hertz.

When you speak, the air begins to vibrate not only at the same frequency as your vocal cords but with energy or volume provided by your breath. This energy or force is called a decibel. A decibel is equal to 20 times the logarithm of the ratio of the sound pressure in the air. If that is as confusing to you as me, let me try an example. A stereo speaker is a paper diaphragm that vibrates. This in turn causes the air around to vibrate at a certain frequency. If you apply more energy and turn the volume up, the speaker does not change its frequency and vibrate faster; it vibrates harder. The more volume, the farther the sound will travel, air molecule by air molecule.

Here are some examples of how loud or how many decibels are generated by various sounds. A whisper or the rustlings of leaves in trees at a distance of five feet are around 10 decibels. A person speaking in a normal tone at three feet is around 60 decibels and someone sitting in the front row of a rock music concert is bombarded with 120 decibels of energy.

The human ear works like a reverse speaker. When sound waves hit the ear, a series of bones within the ear vibrate at the same rate as these sounds, striking the ear drum, becoming audible to us. The human ear does not hear all ranges of sounds. Human beings normally hear sounds ranging between 20 and 20,000 Hertz . Dogs can hear sounds at higher frequencies than us, hence the "silent" dog whistle. This is the ultrasonic range. I am more concerned with what used to be called sub-sonic or infrasonic sounds, as they are known today.

Why do we not hear sounds below 20 Hertz? One reason for this might be because it would drive us crazy. Many of our internal organs like our stomachs and circulatory system vibrate at subsonic frequencies when they function. How would you like to go through life listening to your pulse throb or stomach gurgle 24 hours a day? The earth itself moves and vibrates slowly. Some people claim to be sensitive to subsonic or infrasonic frequencies that help them predict earthquakes.

Scientists have installed infrasonic devices in satellites to help them measure disturbances in the atmosphere like nuclear test detonations.

Scientists have also found that elephants both hear and generate infrasonic sounds. They use this ability to hear sounds as diverse as raindrops striking the ground several miles away or to communicate with another elephant some distance away. Infrasonic sound waves at high decibel levels can have strange effects on the human body.

In the mid-1990s Vic Tandy, an engineer from Coventry University was working late in his laboratory. As he worked he began feeling a strange sense of uneasiness and anxiety. It grew until he was sweating and shivering with fear. Suddenly he saw a gray figure appear out of the corner of his eye. When he turned to face it, the figure vanished. Tandy gathered his belongings and left hurriedly. He returned the next day and began work as usual. He had brought a fencing foil (one of his hobbies) with him. He put the sword in a vice to do some work on it. He left for a short time and returned. When he did, he saw the tip of the sword vibrating wildly.

Being an engineer, Tandy began looking for an explanation for this phenomenon. He had access to various energy recording devices. He found that a heavy-duty exhaust fan that had just been installed was not completely fastened to the wall. Its was vibrating at a frequency of around 19 cycles per second. Like an echo chamber, the walls in the room focused the infrasonic sounds at a spot next to Tandy's work area.

If infrasonic vibrations are generated at high decibel levels they do have strange effects on human beings. They can cause the person to feel unexplained anxiety, fear and a sensation of being watched. Infrasonics can even cause hallucinations. The inner fluid of the human eyeball will begin to vibrate when exposed to sound waves of 18 Hertz. This can cause glowing or dark images to appear at the edge of someone's vision. In order to have these effects the infrasonic vibrations must be produced at a high volume, nearly 80 decibels to produce these effects. This is nearly the same volume as a loud rock concert. Large concert organs can generate high volumes of infrasonic vibrations. This may explain the shiver you get when you attend church or concert recitals.

Tandy took some measuring devices to several locations in Britain that had a reputation for being haunted. In two locations he detected significant levels of subsonic vibrations. At one of the haunted buildings the infrasonic vibrations were caused by a wind tunnel operating the basement. This caused the whole house to vibrate at subsonic levels. In the case of Tandy's laboratory, the sounds were generated at high volumes by a large industrial fan. Many haunted buildings do not have electricity or the machinery necessary to generate the appropriate vibrations.

Tandy and others speculate that natural forces can generate high volume infrasonic sounds. This could happen in an abandoned building with a broken or cracked window. In a high wind storm, the glass could vibrate and generate these sounds. If this window was located at the end of a long hallway the sounds would then be amplified as it echoed off the walls. This would take quite a bit of energy. And it does not explain all hauntings. Tandy did not detect infrasonic vibrations in all of the haunted locations he visited.

As both skeptics and believers will admit, this is natural phenomenon can be measured and defined. It will certainly explain away many hauntings, much to the relief of the house holders. This will allow investigators to concentrate on locations where natural explanations cannot be found. All parties should also admit that although infrasonic sound is entirely natural, it is also rare. I would suggest that the skeptics not write off a haunting as infrasonic sound until they have detected it with scientific instruments.

Summoning the dead through music?

Ghost hunting is a passive and re-active discipline. By

that I mean paranormal investigators spend their time going to haunted locations and waiting for the ghosts or paranormal events to come to them. That does not mean that ghost hunters would not prefer to summon ghosts. That is the great draw of practices like seances, you can conjure or summon the supernatural. Of course the stereotypical problems with psychics is that some of them are frauds and others are deluded. How do you separate the hucksters from the honest?

There have been many scientific attempts to do this. Most people are unaware of the fact that Thomas Edison attempted to do just this. Edison is arguably the greatest inventor of the Industrial age; with over 1,000 patents to his credit. In the October 1920 issue of *Scientific American,* the 72-year-old Edison outlined his theory, which goes something like this, *If* our personalities survive after death, then they should retain memory and a desire to communicate with the living. The spirit entity should also be able to affect matter in doing so. If this is possible, then we should be able to build a machine capable of recording their existence and communication. Edison lived another 11 years after the article was published but was not able to perfect his machine.

Some people believe that the later finding of Electronic Voice Phenomena or EVP first documented in 1959 by Friedrich Jurgenson is proof that Edison was looking for. Jurgenson and others have found that placing a tape recorder in a quiet or haunted location can result in anomalous recordings of either voices or strange sounds that were not heard by the person making the recording while they were sitting there. I have had some success with EVP and I have listened to some tapes of what purport to be ghostly voices. I think that some of these may be the result of hum from the tape recorder motor or the recorder nay have even picked up radio broadcasts. Some of this depends on the quality of the recorder and tape.

Although EVP is an exciting phenomenon, it is still passive. What if we had a device or instrument that would summon spirits. What if certain sounds drew spirits, like high pitched noises drew dogs or ultraviolet light drew certain types of insects? Have you ever rubbed a finger along the wet rim of a glass to hear it "hum", or filled a glass with water and hit it with a spoon to listen to the tone? You may have been calling the spirits, or so people used to believe.

In 1743 Richard Pockridge, invented what he called and Angelic Organ. This device consisted of a permanent set of perfectly tuned wine glasses. Pockridge and his instrument perished in a fire, but a man who attended one of his concerts built an improved model. The admirer was Benjamin Franklin, who was in England at the time as a diplomatic representative of the American Colonies. Franklin liked the sound of the glass music. Rather than having a set of glasses sitting upright, he designed a horizontal rod with a series of glass bowls of varying sizes nested within each other, attached to the spinning rod. The rod spun around in a circle so that the musician touched the bowls to generate sounds. When it was perfected he called it the Armonica, which was the Italian word for harmony.

The armonica was an instant hit in England of the 1760s. When Franklin returned home to America the invention was just as popular. He surprised with wife by playing it when he first returned home. She thought that she had heard the sound of Heaven's music, come down to earth.

During the Revolutionary War, Franklin returned to Europe as America's representative to the French Court. Since most of diplomacy hinges upon pleasantries, Franklin brought his armonica. They were both an instant hit. Thousands of armonicas were produced and sold across Europe. At least 300 works of classical music were written for the glass armonica. The most famous composers associated with the Armonica are Mozart and Beethoven, Hayden and Richard Strauss; all wrote pieces of music for it. Some compositions were written for patrons like Marie Antoinette. The armonica developed a reputation for being able to soothe all kinds of mental illnesses and bring people closer to heaven by it's music. This brought it to the attention of various Great Thinkers and philosophers, including Franz Mesmer.

Mesmer is the father of the psychological science of what is known today as hypnotism. The lines between "natural" sciences like physics and astronomy and "social" sciences like philosophy did not exist at that time. Mesmer was intrigued with a newly discovered natural phenomenon called magnetism. He believed that there was a force called animal magnetism that flowed from one person to another. Mesmer believed that this magnetic field could be channeled in such a way that one person could control or influence another person, putting them in a trance. This is the origin of the word Mesmerism. He believed that it could be aided by the use of magnets. He prescribed cures that included laying in large bathtubs filled with magnets followed by the transmission of animal magnetism from the doctor to patient by rituals involving crystal gazing and the sound of music played on the armonica.

Benjamin Franklin knew Mesmer in Paris and probably attended Mason Lodge meetings with him. As a study commissioned by King Louis XVI, Franklin and other notable scientists of the day watched Mesmer try and cure Franklin's gout. They concluded that Mesmer was probably more successful by virtue of his ritual and salesmanship than his use of magnets and magic. Mesmer remained popular with the French elite for some time but eventually fell from grace.

Although the armonica was reputed to be beneficial to the listener, it was also suspected of causing depression in its players. A medical text written in 1798 recommended against listening or playing the armonica because it could lead to disorders of the blood or even suicide. Far from being uplifting, the sound of the armonica was supposed to be melancholy. It was even thought to summon the spirits of the dead, especially if played at midnight. This is far different from its earlier comparison with the music of heaven. This campaign of depression and death surrounding the armonica led to its downfall as a popular musical instrument by the middle of the 19th century.

There are only two armonica makers in the world today and only a handful of armonica players. One modern armonica player is William Wilde Zeitler. Zeitler lives in Puget Sound and taught himself to play. He recently appeared with the Seattle Philharmonic Orchestra. He has given several concerts and plays at private events. Despite the warnings of 18th and 19th Century physicians he has not yet had a ghost summoned to his presence by his playing.
If you are interested in the story of the armonica or the sound of its music visit Zeitler's web site at www.glassarmonica.com.

The Dark Side of Spiritualism

This is my second book on ghosts and legends. I have visited several dozen haunted properties and talked with hundreds of people. One thing I had hoped would change from the first book to the second was the reception I received from people. Most people I talk to are polite and interested. Some are happy to have someone rational to tell their stories to. It reassures them that they are not isolated. Even if people do not believe, most are polite when they tell me they do not want to discuss ghosts or haunted houses. There are a small percentage of people who I encounter that are definitely not polite. They consider discussing ghosts and haunted houses a disreputable conversation. Especially if it is a house that has been owned by the same family for generations.

Why is it considered bad manners or some kind of family shame to have an ancestor remain behind as a ghost? Part of this attitude is a matter of education and changing times. At this time there is a great amount of speculation and research into spiritual and paranormal matters. This kind of an open forum is a recent social phenomenon. Discussions of the supernatural have cycled between open and closed attitudes. We have just come out of a very long, intense anti-spiritual atmosphere brought on by events in the late 19th and early 20th century.

For thousands of years people have believed in ghosts and a spirit world where the living and dead can communicate with each other. This has been reinforced by the doctrine of many of the world's religions. In the western world of Europe and North America these beliefs were gradually challenged over time. With the coming of the Age of Enlightenment in the 18th and early 19th Centuries, belief in ghosts and the supernatural gradually receded as scientific skepticism looked at past superstitions. Despite the distrust of the supernatural, ghosts and their stories continued, silently in the background of polite society.

In the late 19th century, along with the growth of the natural sciences there was a growing movement to study spiritualism and the supernatural through scientific means. This led to the founding of societies of psychical research in Europe and America as well as the founding of several spiritual churches in the late 19th Century. At that time there were several often-contradictory theories of ghosts and ghostly phenomena that amounted nearly to a mania.

American Spiritualist Church

Part of the current mistrust many Americans have for the paranormal and people who are interested in it are a direct result of the rise and fall of the American Spiritualist Church, which means, the Fox sisters. In 1848 The Fox family of Hydesville NY noticed some very strange things. Their daughter Kate seemed to be followed by ghostly raps and cracks. Kate's mother began speaking with the ghostly noise maker and established a rapping code. When questions were asked the ghost responded with 1 rap for yes and 2 raps for no. A series of questions revealed that the ghost haunting Kate was a peddler who was murdered in the house by the previous owners. Fearing future hauntings the Fox's sent Kate to stay with her sister in Rochester. Shortly after her move the noises resumed in the new location. This time it was the ghost of Kate's grandfather. Other Fox sister's developed mediumistic powers.

Kate's sister Margaret was sent to stay with her brother in Hydesville. While she was there she too was followed by strange ghostly raps. A few years later, Leah Fox developed her own supernatural powers. By 1849 Mrs. Fox had Kate and Margaret brought to Rochester, NY where she jointed them and began exhibiting them to the curious. By 1850 the girls were nationally famous and P.T. Barnum, who coined the expression, "*There's a sucker born every minute*", put the girls on display in his museum in New York City. The Fox's were visited by people ranging from the poor and curious to the wealthy and nobility when they went on a European tour in 1871. Soon people of all walks of life and social status regularly attended seances on a weekly basis.

There are social scientists who have tried to explain the reason why spiritualism was embraced by people so passionately in Europe and America. Several large Spiritualist Churches sprang up. These in turn sponsored smaller franchise ministries ordaining ministers by mail order. These ministers varied in quality and honesty. Some of them were sincere churchmen and women who preached a mix of traditional Christianity with a mix of talk of ghosts and manifestations of ghosts and spirits. Others were hucksters and crooks, concerned with duping their parishioners with phony magic shows in exchange for money.

In addition to the rapping noises the Fox's and others produced a variety of physical effects that were later called Physical Mediumship. Physical mediums became proficient at rapping tables, raising them, and making gramophone trumpets levitate or producing spirit voices. Later they introduced spirit boxes, where more noises and even solid ghosts would exit. Many guests at seances would be surprised with an apport, which is a personal object lost by the guest that the "spirits" cause to appear. The apport would usually appear in the customer's lap. Physical mediums also produced a strange glowing substance called Ectoplasm, which was supposed to be a physical manifestation of spirit energy. Most of this was a mixture of stage magic tricks, sleight of hand and the use of skilled henchmen.

As time went on the mediums and phony spiritualists had

to resort to larger and more elaborate tricks to impress their followers. Many of them became arrogant and convinced they would not be caught. In 1888 Margaret Fox made a confession (paid for by skeptics) that she and her sisters had faked all of their seances. All good (and some not so good things) come to an end. In the early 20th century researchers discredited many psychics and spiritualists. Spirit photographs were shown to be fakes; physical mediums were exposed and the novelty eventually wore out. The large monolithic churches quickly disappeared. After this, there was such a backlash of public opinion that for most people, particularly older people anything having to do with spirituality smacks of ignorance, superstition and disputability.

This does not mean that spiritualist churches are not still around. M. Lamar Keene wrote about his own experiences as a spiritual con man in his book *The Psychic Mafia.* Keene described a nationwide network of phony psychics who would trade information about clients in return for a percentage of any fees or donations made. He describes many of the tricks used phony psychics ranging from mind reading, to the floating spirit trumpet to how ectoplasm is made. After writing his book, Keene has had to move several times because of death threats.

To many readers it probably seems that I am taking a stand against psychics and mediums. This is not true. I am concerned that you, the readers do not become victims. I have met several psychics and shamans over the years. Most of them have been sincere and dedicated to their spiritual powers and growth. How do you tell the difference between the phony and professional? Probably the single greatest way to tell the difference is money. Most honest mediums charge a nominal fee. The fee usually compensates them for lost work, gas or other inconveniences. I would watch out for very high fees and I myself would be wary of people who told me that my money is cursed and the only way to remove the curse is by paying them money or giving it to a church they know of…

Physical mediumship was the most famous form of

séance performed in the large spiritualist churches. It was not the oldest form of spiritual channeling or seances. For centuries people across the world have practiced what is now called mental mediumship or scrying. Perhaps because the physical mediums and their supporters ignored mental mediumship it was not discredited or attacked as heavily.

The word scry comes from the English word *descry*, which means, "*to make out dimly*" or "*to perceive something that is obscured*". Whether they are sitting in controlled settings like their own parlor or in a haunted house, mediums attempt to do just this. A mental medium communicates with the dead by inducing a trance through staring at a shiny object such as a crystal ball, glass of water or even a polished fingernail. Staring at the object supposedly frees their minds from everyday concerns and allows them to perceive or scry paranormal entities or energy.

According to several eminent skeptics and scientists, this kind of mediumship is an example of a hypnotic trance that frees up stored human brain potential. The ability to process a few pertinent facts from large amounts of useless information into the answer of a problem may seem like supernatural insight. People communicate by body language, it may be that a medium would subconsciously observe the language of the customer and formulate a complete "vision" that would be insightful to the customer.

This is part of the problem that frustrates for both psychic researchers and the honest psychics alike. How do you verify the truth of their visions? Where people claim to have psychic mind reading abilities, it is relatively easy to test their claims under controlled settings. How do you test messages from the dead? Sometimes you can, and sometimes you cannot. I prefer to look at the growing ability of science to tell us what is NOT paranormal, like infrasonics, infrared photography and skilled researchers as a very good thing for people who believe in the possible existence of the paranormal. That is because they can help us all separate out the reasonable and known from the true unknown and then leave us with those few cases where we cannot find a mundane reason for strange phenomenon, which will then allow us to say, yes this is a spiritual or ghostly happening.

If anyone is curious about his or her own psychic abilities it is easy to try scrying. It is best to try this in a dark room to minimize distractions. There should be as little outside sensory input as possible. Some people believe that it is necessary to begin with chanting or burning sacred herbs. This ritual may help people achieve a trance; if they believe in the ritual it may act like a pre-hypnotic suggestion. Other people believe that it is best to have no distractions like music or incense. Next fix your attention on a shiny object. This can be a candle flame, a bowl of water, a crystal or even a polished fingernail. Concentrate on the shiny object for several minutes without straining yourself. Just try to shut out your awareness of the outside world.

After a few minutes you should begin to see visions in the surface. They may be random visions or they may actually tell stories. Try this for between 10 and 15 minutes. If this does not happen the first time, do not be disappointed. Scrying requires internal discipline and concentration. Try it several times. If you do have success, try to ask questions and receive answers; and record what is happening. Again, skeptics will claim that this is just an occurrence of self-hypnosis. I do not dispute this, but I am amazed at how insightful some people can be or how many facts they never knew can surface. Sometimes it cannot be explained away as forgotten memories or heightened awareness.

Until someone comes up with definite answers I will keep looking for them myself and I encourage all of the readers to do the same themselves

Jeff Davis

Works Consulted

Books

Finucane, R. C.
1996 *Ghosts Appearances of the Dead & Cultural Transformation.* Prometheus Books, Amherst, New York.

Jackson, Robert
1992 *Great Mysteries.* Smithmark Publishers Inc., New York, NY.

Keene, M. Lamar
1997 The Psychic Mafia, Prometheus Books, Amherst, NY.

McCutcheon, Marc
1989, *The Compass in Your Nose and Other Astonishing Facts about Humans*, Penguin Books, NY.

Rawcliffe, D. H.
1959 *Illusions and Delusions of the Supernatural and Occult*, Dover Publications, New York.

Schmidt, Jean-Claude
1998 *Ghosts in the Middle Ages*, University of Chicago Press, Chicago, Il.

Smyth, Frank
1992 "The ghosts in the machine," *Mysteries of the Mind, Space and Time*, p 887- 872, H.S. Stuttman INC., Westport, CN.

Spencer, John and Anne Spencer
1992 *The Encyclopedia of Ghosts and Spirits.* Headline Book Publishing PLC, London.

Spencer, John and Tony Wells
1996 *Ghostwatching The Ghosthunters' Handbook.* Virgin Books, London.

Randi, James
1987 *Flim-Flam!,* Prometheus Books, Amherst, NY.

Underwood, Peter
1986 *The Ghosthunter's Guide.* Javelin Books, New York, NY.

Periodicals

Matthews, Robert
30 June 1998 "Science wrecks a good ghost story", the *Daily News*, Vancouver BC, Canada.

Payne, Katherine
1989 "Elephant Talk", *National Geographic* 176(2), p. 264.

Internet resources

Moir, Patricia
12 December 1998 "Opera of glasses: Rare glass instrument inspires musician," the *Eastside Journal*, www.eastsidejournal.com

Zeitler, William W.
December 1998 "The glass armonica," *www.glassarmonica.com*

The following books and internet sites were consulted throughout this book

Floyd, E. Randall

1993 *Ghost Lights and Other Encounters with the Unknown.* August House Publisher, Inc., Little Rock.

Hauk, Dennis William

1996 *The National Directory of Haunted Places.* Penguin Books Inc., New York.

Helm, Mike

1983 *Oregon's Ghosts and Monsters.* Rainy Day Press, Eugene, OR.

Hills, Tim, editor

Resonance from the Festival, Portland, OR. This is the McMenamins monthly newsletter.

MacDonald, Margaret Read

1995 *Ghost Stories from the Pacific Northwest.* August House Publishers, INC., Little Rock Arkansas

Meyers, Arthur

1986 *The Ghostly Register.* Contemporary Books, INC. Chicago, IL.

1993 *A Ghosthunter's Guide to Haunted Landmarks, Parks, Churches, and Other Public Places.* Contemporary Books, Contemporary Publishing Company, Chicago, IL.

Internet Resources

GST Data Services' Web o f Intrigue: *wysiwkyg://28http://halloween.gstis.net/index.html.*

Ghost Stories from Around the World: *http://www.sitemart.com/ghost/18145.htm.*

Ghosts of North Portland Web site: *http://www.hevanet.com/herberb/ghosts/mohawk.htm.*

International Ghost Hunter Society: *http://www.aone.com.*

McMenamins website; http*://www.mcmemamins.com*

Portland Halloween net: *http://halloween.gstis.net.html*

Richard Senate's home page*: www.aim.tj/JAM/ghost/ghost.htm*

Spectre Search Home Page: *http://web2.arimail.net/~spectre1.sprportl.html*

University of Cheltenham, Student Parapsychology Society: *http://www.chelt.ac.uk/su/sps/haunt.htm*

Index

To order more copies of **Ghost, *Critters* & Sacred Places of Washington and Oregon** and **Ghosts and *Strange* Critters of Washington and Oregon** please complete the form below and mail check or money order to Norseman Ventures, at PO Box 4803, Vancouver, WA 98662

* Sales Tax applies **only** to Washington Residents

Item	**No.**	**Price**	**Tax***	**Total**
Ghost and Strange Critters of WA and OR		X $10.95	+ 80 ea	
Ghosts, Critters & Sacred Places of WA and OR		X $12.95	+$.95 ea	
Shipping and Handling on the first book only				$2.50
Shipping and Handling for each additional book			$1.00 each	
			Total Amount Enclosed	$

ShipTo:

Name ____________________

Address ____________________

City/State/Zip Code ____________________

Phone Number ____________________

About the Author

Jeff Davis was born in Vancouver, Washington in 1962. According to family tradition he is related to his namesake, Jefferson Davis, President of the Confederacy. Jeff is an Army brat who grew up playing in and around the Vancouver Barracks. This led to an interest in the military and history. Late night horror movies led to an interest in ghosts, mythology and archaeology.

After a three year enlistment in the US Army, Jeff returned to college where he earned a Bachelor's degree in Anthropology. For several years Jeff worked for the US Forest service as an archaeologist on the Gifford Pinchot, the Boise, the Umatilla, and Mt. Hood National Forests.

In 1995 Jeff and his wife moved to England for a year where he earned his MA in Archaeology at the University of Sheffield. His thesis topic was the lifestyle of the Viking settlers in Greenland. That is where he received the inspiration for his publishing company name, Norseman Ventures.

In addition to his work as a freelance archaeologist and researching books on the paranormal, Jeff is planning on travelling to Greenland and producing a multi-media CD on the Vikings who settled there.